architecturetomorrow

General Editor: Anne Zweibaum-Longérinas

Coordinating Editor: Christine Marchandise

Design: Christian Kirk-Jensen / Danish Pastry Design

Picture Editor: Gabriella Pessoa De Queiroz

Copy Editor: Natasha Edwards

Photoengraving: Eurografica

English Translation: John Tittensor

Edigroup / Terrail, Paris 2005
25, rue Ginoux 75015 Paris, France

ISBN: 2-87939-286-1

Printed in Italy

architecture
tomorrow
francis rambert

TERRAIL

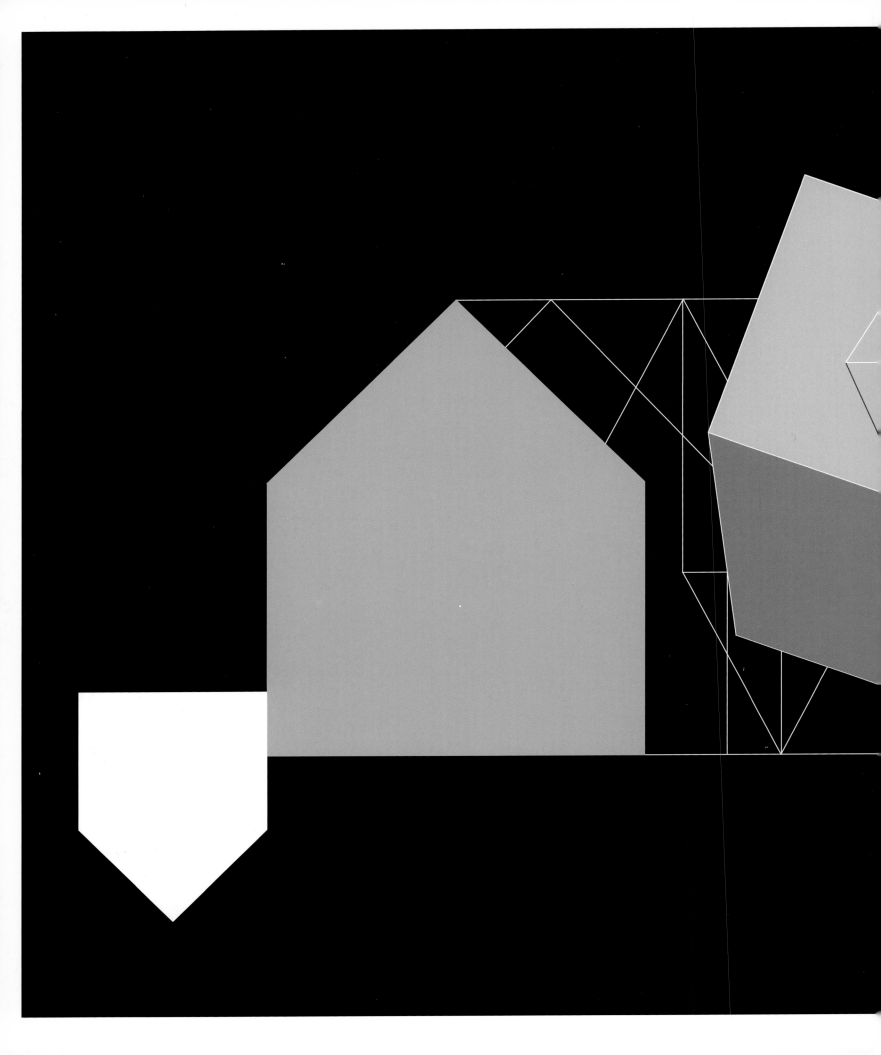

a turning point

Hybridisation is what the opening of the new century is all about, and the result is alternatives to globalisation: a proliferation of buildings that are unique and specific, and not ashamed to use glamour to change our perceptions; and of manifesto-style "installations" that take architecture to the brink of contemporary art.

chapter one →

1

"HIGH-TECH" VS "LOW-TECH"

1. **Norman Foster's hyper-sophisticated Swiss Re tower in London.** Nicknamed "The Gherkin", this is the new emblem of the City, London's business district: rising like a missile from an underground silo, it brings a totally new approach to the office building with its ascending succession of atriums.

Facing page.
2. **Stuhlmacker, Parasite, 2004.** So called because it has no legal existence, the "Parasite" is a wooden mini-tower Korteknie & Stuhlmacher have installed on the roof of an old warehouse in Rotterdam's dockland. This temporary but habitable construction is now a familiar part of the Dutch city's skyline.

While we wait for the big international rendezvous, London is offering an amazing duet: a stately dialogue between two iconic buildings in the heart of the City. On one side is the headquarters of that archetypal institution, Lloyd's of London, and on the other the brand new Swiss Re tower. Richard Rogers' modules-and-pipes machine, the service-industry cathedral that in 1986 incurred the wrath of Prince Charles by defying St Paul's; and Norman Foster's new, all-curves tower, immediately nicknamed "The Gherkin". One insures, the other reinsures or, more precisely, reassures. Twenty years separate the two.

Different eras, different forms. The high-tech fashion is well and truly past, but looking harder we see a trend to complexity with a dash of conviviality. Right angles, blocks and bars are no longer absolute masters. The curve, and even more so the free form, have taken over our contemporary landscape. Gone is the fatality of banality. Once there was "The Egg", brainchild of French architect André Bruyère, who declaimed to all and sundry that "architecture is the way you mould love around a constraint." Laid (on paper) in 1978, the egg – a tower – was supposed to hatch in the middle of New York. Today's architecture enjoys rounding things off, when it is not striving for disappearance, or for the blur effect with its wiping-out of the frontiers of the real.

In the eternal palimpsest of the city, everything is already there, part of the mutation of a world hungry for information and still careless about its ecological balances. From the media skyscrapers and Wi-Fi spaces to "ecologically correct" buildings, architecture is the reflection of a society as paradoxical as it is dissatisfied; and maybe even more the sign of the changes and questionings of the modern world. As Mies van der Rohe reminded us, "Architecture is a historical process, one

Could it be that the ghost of Aldous Huxley is coming back to life in the Middle Kingdom? Scheduled for 2010, the Universal Exhibition in Shanghai makes no bones about the brave new world to come: Better City, Better Life. It might sound like an ad man's slogan, but that's the theme chosen by one of the world's most hectic metropolises. What's going to be on show in this endlessly burgeoning city? Will the theme prove capable of reviving the Universal Exhibition concept, born in London in 1851 with Paxton's Crystal Palace but looking pretty worn since Seville in 1992. Can we expect new kinds of architecture for new lifestyles?

2

belonging to its time." Our time is the time of the "already there", with architecture turned towards transformation, extension and restructuring: in Europe, at least, this is hardly a period of ravenous consumption of land.

Möbius & Co.

One sign of the times is a certain kind of shift. Architecture is expressing itself less via structure and more via texture. The skin has overtaken the skeleton. Even when the skeleton is still very much there – Herzog & de Meuron's Prada building in Tokyo, Rudy Ricciotti's Dance Centre in Aix-en-Provence, Rem Koolhaas's Seattle Library, Jean Nouvel's Agbar Tower in Barcelona, Massimiliano Fuksas's Fiera di Milano – it is the overall image that prevails in these key works of the early 21st century. Mighty mesh, mammoth pixellisation or organic universe: skeleton and texture are indissociable for the creation of effects that are bringing architecture closer to the plastic arts. In its own small way, the Kengo Kuma bamboo house – a house with two skins and glass walls filled with feathers, at the foot of the Great Wall of China (2003) – magnificently illustrates this fusion.

If we go along with artist Roberto Matta's statement, "Painting has one foot in architecture and the other in dreams", it would be tempting to suggest that architecture is trying to have the best of both worlds: between immanence and exuberance, between the demands of the discipline and freedom of formal expression, and with poetry thrown in, if necessary.

There is no shortage of metaphorical effects, either. The wave (and even its foam) is very big and the cloud is peeping through in various present and future projects. Then there are the fold, origami, strip and other envelope-inflected movements, which constitute not simply a trend, but a thoroughgoing mutation. The Möbius strip is finding disciples everywhere – Ben van Berkel, Christian de Portzamparc, NL Architects, Shishei Endo and others – in a world given over to twists and turns and circumvolutions: continuity of form and ground for creation of new spaces, new sensations.

What is notable is how the spirit of Pampulha, Brazil, Oscar Niemeyer's church of the 1950s – a small, undulatory masterpiece – still pervades an architectural imagination strongly drawn, as it happens, to concepts coming out of the rhizome and dissemination. Let's not forget that in the Parc de la Villette in Paris, Bernard Tschumi dotted a brownfield site – the French capital's former abattoirs – with his red "follies": a building broken up into 23 separate entities. And fifteen years later, in 2004, in their model for the renewal of Les Halles in the heart of Paris, Rem Koolhaas and his OMA team came up with a project based on the notion of fragmentation in the form of various "emergences": coloured towers that would dynamise the public space, while bringing light to the inside.

LUXURY AS ONE OF THE FINE ARTS
3>5. Herzog & de Meuron's Prada store on Omote-Sando, Tokyo's Champs-Elysées. Here a building/showcase has actually found a way of creating vacant space in one of the world's most expensive cities: a little square set on the roof of the basement. Hybrid and organic, the six-storey building brings enormous inventiveness to its marriage of effective retailing and corporate philosophy. A veritable little jewel, its load-bearing facade features interplay between flat, convex and concave diamond shapes. The look is totally Herzog & de Meuron, the firm having designed the project down to the last detail, from the sophisticated frontages through to the fibreglass interiors. The diamond grid covers every square inch of this little glass tower, including the roof.

4

5

Graphic (facadewise) in the 1970s, anecdotal (and historicist) in the 80s, and eclectic in the 90s, architecture has become progressively more and more topographical and geographical. It wants to be one with the soil and, more generally, with its environment.

We've gone beyond integration to the stage of fusion. Which means that the term "contextual" is no longer really appropriate for projects that tend to create their own landscape and manufacture their own logic. Some go as far as constructing a new topography, like the great glass fault line cut through the Ewha University campus in Seoul (Dominique Perrault, project, 2004), the geological architecture of the Cantabrian museum at Santander (Mansilla & Tunon, project, 2003), and the artificial hill against the city wall imagined by Vincente Guallart at Denia in Spain (project, 2002) for housing a multipurpose centre; not to mention the vegetalised tumulus suggested by Jean Nouvel for the Japan Guggenheim. So architecture is moving towards Land Art, whose major form of expression is works on the scale of landscape, such as Christo's pink islands and Robert Smithson's *Spiral Jetty*.

Spanish critic Manuel Gausa has neatly termed the results "Land arch".

Hybridization of form and concept

Stances have changed fast over the past forty years, with the end of ideology and the fall of the Berlin Wall in 1989 bringing a new state of affairs. At the end of the 1970s there was an abyss separating the heroes of pastiche, and postmodernism in general, from the knights of high-tech, out to show the truth of the structure the way some people flaunt their muscles. One side claimed to be protecting the city, the other advocated architecture in its most expressively efficient form.

Positions are less radical today and things are more complex or, rather, more subtle. The era of the white cube museum and the shoebox auditorium seems well and truly past – as does that of postmodernism, which had reached the end of its cul-de-sac. We're into the age of hybridization of forms and concepts and of the move into what anthropologist Marc Augé has called "supermodernity".

In a single century architecture has been

through two revolutions: at the beginning of the 20th century, the arrival of reinforced concrete brought a new kind of structure and shaped the face of Modernism; and at the end, the arrival of the computer in architects' studios shook design approaches to their foundations.

Japanese architect Kazuyo Sejima, known for his work on transparency and immateriality, nonetheless stresses the importance of the "reality" of architecture: "At a time when people communicate via different media in nonphysical space, it is the responsibility of architects to create real spaces for direct, physical communication." The issue of the static as opposed to the fluid is looming larger. Kazuyo's winning proposal for the EPFL polytechnic in Lausanne, Switzerland (2004), offers a highly poetic version of this idea of interpersonal communication. A sheet seems set to cover the campus with disconcerting lightness. There are buildings that undulate and rise, while all remain very close to the soil and close to the lake. The idea is similar to Toyo Ito's project for a "layer park" (Hakata Bay, 2005) at Fukuoka in southern Japan,

MINIMUM LANDSCAPE IMPACT
6. **The Ewha University fault line, cut by Dominique Perrault into the heart of Seoul.** All glass walls, "Campus Valley" is a multifunctional space for 20,000 students. Playing with the topography of the site, Perrault's strategy of concealment centres on an incision 250 metres long and 20 metres wide.

6

7

whose architecture creates undulations via the movement and other modulations stamped on an immense structure of plant-covered reinforced concrete.

Post-accident civilization

The world had barely moved into the new millennium when it was stunned by the collapse of the Twin Towers in Manhattan. Architecture, that abstract icon of economic power, was the victim of an unprecedented terrorist attack. The events of the morning of 11 September 2001 went far beyond those that had previously plunged specific sites into mourning: the Munich Olympic stadium in 1972 or the Temple at Amritsar in India in 1984. Architecture was KO'd, like an America reliving the nightmare of Pearl Harbor. Some 3,000 dead buried under 1.6 million tons of debris. The very next day the American architect Daniel Libeskind took it on himself to declare: "From now on, architecture will never be the same."

But wasn't architecture already not quite the same? Hadn't we already moved into a post-accident civilization? The Chernobyl disaster of 1986 had left its traces far beyond the

borders of Belorussia, as witnessed by the "Ecology of fear", Mike Davis' Book (1998) or by "Ce qui arrive" ("What Happens") exhibition at the Fondation Cartier in Paris in 2002. Designed by philosopher Paul Virilio, this exhibition offered "a conscious reappropriation of what has not been thought about", as Claude Parent's former associate called for the creation of an accident museum. The glamorising of dramatic situations may have seemed somewhat spooky, but the images spoke for themselves, from the nuclear mushroom to the stock market crash and the derailing of the German high-speed train. Virilio directed our attention to "the structure falling apart: deconstruction", with a photo of the Kobe earthquake showing those typically Asian, elevated urban motorways tipped over, wiped out. Troubling, too, in the same exhibition, to see another photo of the earthquake that looks for all the world like a forerunner of a different kind of harbour station, built by FOA at Yokohama in 2002 – except that there the ground covers instead of slipping away.

Kobe generated reactions, conscious or otherwise. One of them was the famous emergency house produced by Shigeru Ban in Japan for those left homeless by the 1995

NEW WAVES ON THE LAKESHORE
7. **Kazuyo Seijima's evanescent structures for the Lausanne Polytechnic (EPFL) in Switzerland.** On the shores of Lake Geneva, the Seijima approach brings splendid lightness and fluidity to the interplay between indoors and outdoors.

ONE WAY OF FITTING IN
8. **Geninasca & Delafortie's footbridge over the Areuse at Boudry, Switzerland.** Just another part of the natural scene. Thirty metres long, this is a geometrical structure whose S-shape and variations in width in no way detract from its unity. Merging beautifully with the surrounding forest, it uses its fir slats to cancel out any distinction between "facade" and "roof".

8

FILTERING SPACE AND LIGHT
9+10. **Japanese architect Kengo Kuma's bamboo house at the foot of the Great Wall of China.** Lynchpin of the luxury "Commune" development, this is a house in search of symbiosis with its mountain setting. The bamboo screen of the facade minimises the impact of a contemporary creation on one of China's heritage shrines, while a curtain helps you frame the view and manage the effects of the sun. The house in fact has a double skin, the bamboo concealing feather-filled glass walls.

earthquake: a fine, enduring example of the sublimation of function. This little house – 16 square metres – made of cardboard tubing and beer crates restored architectural dignity to survival accommodation. This building, which also proved its worth in Turkey after the Istanbul earthquake in 1999, is as easy to take down as it is to build, and its components are recyclable, showing a fine mix of aesthetics and economy of means.

This crucial decade astride two centuries (1995-2005) had its own keywords: the "urban fabric" was filled out with other, even more biological notions, such as "urban substance" and "opened plasma". At the same time, there had never been so much talk about complexity ; about mobility, with the coming of the Segway for personal urban transport the "wearable car (by Toyota) and the "flashmob" (urban happenings organised by SMS and other mobile phone messaging systems); about ethics – "Less aesthetics, more ethics" demanded the Venice Architecture Biennale, directed by Massimiliano Fuksas in 2000; about ecology, with the rise of "sustainable development" and its corollary, "urban regeneration"; and about sensuality and multisensoriality. It should be said, too, that this same decade was marked by the appearance of fresh talents. China's phenomenal growth brought new names to the fore, among them Qingyun Ma and Deshaus in Shanghai, and Shu Pei, Cui Kai and Qi Xin in Beijing.

Sense and sensuality

Doubtless wearied by having produced so much "gesture" – not always elegant or really appropriate – architecture has come to see itself in a new light, that of a culture of the specific. This has entailed getting rid of the notion of style, together with neutralising the question of form, in the interests of foregrounding approach – contextual or conceptual, according to the circumstances. Sustainable is desirable.

Having exorcised the demons of the 1960s-70s clean slate, architects were better equipped to espouse a new agenda.

Less gesture, more specificity: such is the line of conduct, not to say the contemporary ethic. Gone is the need to give the top of a highrise building a Neoclassical pediment, as Philip Johnson had done – not without a touch of humour – in Manhattan when postmodernism was reaching fever pitch (AT&T Tower, New York 1982). Nor is it appropriate to import a formalist vocabulary into a historic urban context. The Macba (Museu d'Art Contemporani de Barcelone) in Barcelona – the "white icebox" as Richard Meier's detractors call it – reeks of pre-prepared architecture, with no surprises and no special savour. One is tempted to borrow painter Mark Rothko's remark on specificity in his text on shapes: "They are unique elements in a unique situation."

The Australian Glenn Murcutt, whose houses are well in phase with landscapes and lifestyle, has the right idea when he speaks of "an architecture appropriate to the place"; while British architect Louisa Hutton (Sauerbruch & Hutton) settles for a useful version of the obvious: "Creating buildings specific to their brief and specific to their site." As simple as that. In other words, there and not elsewhere: the end of the standard recipe, then, and of the universally exportable model.

Thus sports stadiums no longer have to look like soup tureens or cooking pots. The stadium at Braga in Portugal, with its distinctive relationship with its site, is resounding proof. With only two grandstands, this is the stadium at Braga and no other. Designed by Souto de Moura (2004), it has a sculptural feel to it on one side so as to meld better with the rock on the other, a technical feat, with its two enormous concrete "tents" that seem to echo of the big sail of Alvaro Siza's Pavilion in Lisbon (1998).

In a more immaterial vein, the appearance at Amiens, in France, of a glass stadium resem-

12

13

SOAKING IT UP
11. **Peter Zumthor's thermal baths in Vals, Switzerland.** Solidly attached to its mountainside, the long building plays with the contrast between the low-key near-austerity of the outside and the luxury feel provided by a similar minimalism indoors. Sound, temperature and lighting provide the visitor with a world of sensory, sensual delights in a marvellously tactile setting.

STONE AND WATER
12>14. **House at Lantian, China, by Ma Qingyun.** A tricky, difficult exercise for the Mada s.p.a.m. architect: a house for his father in the Jade Valley near Xi'an, using pure geometry and such time-honoured materials as locally quarried stone and woven bamboo to cover the inside walls. This rectangular, two-storey house includes an interior courtyard and a swimming pool extending along the entire length of the plot.

14

bling an enormous greenhouse (Chaix & Morel, 1999), makes perfect sense in the context of the marshy, canal-threaded fenland around it, while also offering a view of one of the most handsome cathedrals in Europe and Auguste Perret's tower. In Germany, Herzog & de Meuron's new 80,000-seat Munich stadium, scheduled to open in 2005, harks back to the history of the site. For the 1972 Olympics Gunther Behnisch and Frei Otto produced one of the masterpieces of sports architecture with a plastic canvas stretched over stays. Thirty years later the Swiss pair have used a fluopolymer membrane for their structure comprising 1,000 diamond-shaped cushions. When inflated it looks not unlike a dirigible.

The same appropriateness is to be found in Jean Nouvel's design for the aquatic centre tower at Le Havre. A double platform – the first at 100 metres, the second at 200 metres – functions as a kind of control tower for craft in movement and provides a panoramic viewpoint over the docks and a balcony overlooking Auguste Perret's city. We could call this a new contextuality. Interestingly, in a reaction to any notion of a "generic city", Herzog & de Meuron get their students at Harvard to do research on city identity.

We are clearly no longer dealing with the genius loci of the 1970s-80s: rather than revealing the "spirit of the place", the aim now is to make the most of it. "I think," comments David Chipperfield, designer of the River and Rowing Museum at Henley-on-Thames (1997), "that what's needed is continuity, and our responsibility is to find the clues to this in memory and context." In this very conservative English town, Chipperfield's minimalism is thoroughly at odds with regionalist thinking: his return to the ridge roof, for example, is considered an act of treason by hardline modernists. Yves Lion's French Embassy in Beirut (2003), built in local stone on the old demarcation line, fits with this rationale of hunting out "clues" in the martyred city.

Looking for meaning does not exclude stimulating the senses. Remember, for example, Philippe Starck's 1989 Asahi building in central Tokyo, with its tall golden flame leaping out of a black, urn-shaped building. This was Starck's (naive) way of creating what he called "fertile surprises", of making cities less boring. More subtly, the Sauerbruch & Hutton duo, designers of the famous GSW building in Berlin – built in 1999, ten years after the fall of the Wall – claimed the right to "a sensual quality" they put excitingly into practice by appeal-

16

ing to all the senses. As they explain, "It's always something to do with materiality and surface, with colours and spatial structuring." A symphony in orange and red, their tall emblem for the new German capital functions as a work of contemporary art, an icon of urban regeneration, in the same way as Norman Foster's reworking of the Reichstag. Sauerbruch & Hutton approach is all the more conspicuous in that they have applied it to briefs for which banality seems to be a universal law: office blocks and industrial structures. While it would be simplistic to label Sauerbruch & Hutton as colourists, they do set out to make their buildings appetising, whatever their function: a ministry, a fire station, a laboratory or a straightforward warehouse.

Another duo, Jean-Marc Ibos and Myrto Vitart – in France, this time – also love combining geometry and colour. Their magnificent extension to the Palais des Beaux-Arts in Lille (1997), a red and gold exhibition space that is the lynchpin of the renovation of the

TENTS IN CONCRETE
15+16. **The stadium at Braga, Portugal, by Edouardo Souto de Moura.** As the kick-off for redevelopment of the city, the stadium backs onto a quarry wall, its concrete merging with the rockface. Inspired by the Roman amphitheatre, this is a dramatic contemporary arena whose central space, between rock and concrete, recalls Piranesi. Matches are played to two grandstands only. Like Alvaro Siza's pavilion in Lisbon, the stadium has two enormous concrete tents, 40 metres tall, sheltering the pitch: an impressive technical achievement.

GREENHOUSE EFFECT
17. Chaix & Morel's La Licorne sports stadium in Amiens, France. A transparent, 12,000-seat arena combining structural simplicity and visual fluidity. Running counter to the standard "cooking pot" model, its incurving, 26-metre-high walls open onto both the playing area and the surrounding landscape: sport staged with enormous elegance. The structure itself contributes a rhythmic energy via the white arches every eight meters along the facades.

19th-century museum, is part of a strategy of recreation of a landscape. Set behind a reappropriated public space, the building becomes part of the interplay of reflection and transparency in a vast wall of glass that gives rise to endless superpositions.

Since then, in 2004, Ibos & Vitart have come up with a matchless hospital building in Paris. The Maison de Solenn, an experimental care centre for teenagers in difficulty, bears no resemblance to a classical health facility, reaching out to the city and to life itself. Streetside, facing the Val de Grâce, the architects have created a 110-metre-long glass origami, whose subtle green tint generates a pleasing ambiguity between the facades and Louis Benech's garden, and between indoors and outdoors. All in all, it marks a sophisticated use of geometry in terms of both building and garden. And the fifth facade – with its large glass screens tipping a wink to Dan Graham – aspires to becoming a rooftop vegetable garden in the heart of the capital.

Transforming the perception of things

Also interested in the idea of "wiping out frontiers", architects Mansilla & Tunon have approached the new museum of contemporary art in the Spanish city of Leon (the Musac,

2004) as "a game of chess in which action is the spatial protagonist". Their plan – a cluster of independent rooms suited to all kinds of exhibitions – is the tool for a dynamic stage set for art, happenings and performances. Orchestrated by 500 prefabricated concrete beams, this distinctive work makes use of colour on its facade to enliven the surrounding urban space.

As isolated as these experiments may be, they still add up to a trend: cities are getting back into colour and the alternative to "stone-tone" is happening. After the attempts at urban "colourisation" in the 70s-80s, with Stanley Tigerman's Library for the Blind in Chicago, César Pelli's "Blue Whale" in Los Angeles and, in particular, in France's new towns – colour is back in force, but not without subtlety. It can take the form of simply tinting the materials, as in Mario Garzanti's little corner building in Brussels' Schaerbeek district (2003): a very simple, plastically pleasing operation offering the beauty of an abstract sculpture in Corten steel.

On a larger scale, Otto Steidle in Munich has undertaken a contextual exercise involving coloured treatment of his facades. In this most Italianate of German cities, with its stucco rendering in pink, pistachio, mauve and lemon yellow, the Wacker Haus housing ensemble (1998) – notable for the fact that it

bestrides a watercourse – is integrated in a series of five perfectly natural steps. In this it is the opposite of the Goetz Collection, a small, extremely minimalist museum built in the same city and at the same period by the Swiss team of Herzog & de Meuron.

Colour at the service of urbanity is also the goal of Ben van Berkel (UN Studio) in his office ensemble in the Dutch new town of Almere. Entitled "La Défense" (2003), the operation is readily distinguishable from the projects on the famous La Défense in western Paris. This city block of offices includes variations in length, height and, above all, colour. The glass panels used are equipped with multicoloured films allowing the facades to change continuously from yellow to blue, red to purple, green to black. Partly inspired by Monet's series of paintings of Rouen Cathedral, these chromatic variations are intended to change people's perception of the density of the ensemble. More than a collection of offices, this is a place: a place permeable to its environment.

Since we're talking about shifts in perception, a remarkable collaboration between an artist and an architect deserves mention. James Turrell's colouring by illumination of the Caisse des Dépôts building in Paris in 2003 represents a conscious search for fresh sensations that adds a whole new dimension to Christian Hauvette's scrupulous architec-

17

18

HOSPITAL AS HOTEL

18+19. **The Maison de Solenn in Paris.** An experimental care centre for teenagers in difficulty. The work of Ibos & Vitart, this glass vessel stands on a long, trapezoidal block opposite the 17th-century Val de Grâce church. The contemporary facade is made up of green-tinted glass panels that increase the feeling of fusion between indoors and outdoors. A highly sophisticated geometrical approach combines the organisation of the building with the composition of Louis Benech's garden.

The building is topped by a terrace protected by large screens of glass, a totally unexpected space offering a 360° view of the French capital. The idea is to give the teenagers a fresh taste for life – and for the city.

19

21

CHROMATIC VARIATIONS
21+22. **La Défense: an office cluster at Almere, Holland.**
Using four strips of different heights and varying length, this office block designed by UN Studio plays equally with density and irregularity. An interesting feature here is the capacity of the facades to change with the sky, owing to the colour films inserted in the glass panels: from yellow to blue, from red or purple to green.

Preceding double-page spread.
A WINNING COMBINATION
20. **MUSAC: Mansilla & Tunon's museum of contemporary art at Leon, Spain.** The museum makes no secret of its intentions as a work of art in its own right. Facades of translucent or coloured glass are an open invitation to the passer-by and dynamise the surrounding public space, while the indoor area makes sophisticated, combinatory use of 500 prefabricated concrete beams. In abandoning the idea of a large open area, the architects have succeeded in creating a flexible space for exhibitions of different kinds and on different scales.

ture. Set on the banks of the Seine, by night this great glass vessel becomes an exhibition space for pictures in movement.

Utility and nobility

If we look at today's so-called "local" architecture – all those little facilities you find in a neighbourhood – the striving for a more agreeable everyday life is tangible. This confirms the notion that there is no such thing as a small project, and that architecture cannot afford to restrict itself to large-scale ventures. The market place is well-known as a subject that has given rise to all sorts of structural exploits: after the market in Royan, France, in the 50s and Jean François Zévaco's concrete "umbrellas" in Casablanca in the 70s, Enric Miralles and Benedetta Tagliabue brought magnificent new life to the genre in Barcelona in 2004. Not far from the cathedral, the eye is caught by an unexpected movement at roof level: the vision of something like a giant butterfly perched on the venerable stones. Here the redevelopment of a local market has provided the opportunity for a superposition that draws attention away from the operation's slightly superficial aspect. The highly assertive

new structure supports a projecting, undulating, headily coloured roof.

Creating after a contemporary manner of Arcimboldo, the Barcelona team imagine a roof (made of fruits and vegetables) which reaches a degree of abstraction by pixelisation.

More discreet and closer in tone to its surroundings, Adelfo Scaranello's project in Arnay-le-Duc in Burgundy (2002) is just as emblematic of an approach based on highlighting a basic, functional town facility in a spirit of simplicity and extreme sensitivity. A lover of contemporary art – he is also the creator, with artist Gloria Friedman, of the Red Cube, a rural gîte at Villars Santenoge also in Burgundy (1994) – the architect entrusted the decoration of the enamel wall panels of the covered market to the painter Marc Camille Chaimowicz. Raised on market days, the panels descend at closing time. When not in use, the building is far from mute, its handsome walls carrying on a fascinating dialogue with the venerable stone buildings around them.

Another interesting example is the Gravilliers market hall at Athis-Mons, in the suburbs of Paris. Carried out by the Berthelier-Fichet-Tribouillet team (BFT, 2001), the project is part of a strategy of total transformation of a site: this is a public space recreated in Corten steel, with the floor designed as a raised, horizontal plate.

Another instance of ennoblement – of turning utilitarian buildings into works of art – is the highly successful aesthetics of the signal box at Basel station in Switzerland. This work by Herzog & de Meuron (1999) stands out through the elegance of a signal box made entirely of thin strips of copper and directly connected to the railway sidings. There are interesting similarities here with Lyon & Du Besset's Médiathèque in Orléans (1994). True, the architectural performance involved may seem less surprising in the case of a cultural building regarded as embodying certain aesthetic values, but this building, with its permeable metal facades that allow for a view of the city, plays on the same parametres: the notion of a signal set at a major intersection, and facades of undulating slivers of metal.

The contemporary art connection

A change of scenery: out of the urban and into the thermal baths at Vals, in the Swiss mountains. Also extremely sober from the exterior, this masterly piece of work by Peter Zumthor (1996) is a monument of sensuality inside.

22

COLOUR AS CONCEPT
23. **The Sedus innovation and development centre at Dogern, Germany, by Sauerbruch & Hutton.** Rising above the roofs of its neighbors, this enormous oblong block plays a positive part in its surroundings. Commissioned to extend the Sebus office-furniture warehouse, the architects used a twenty-colour palette to play down the sheer mass of the building. And this wasn't all: with its hipped roof and highly distinctive geometry, the small building that actually houses the innovation and development centre sets out to establish a relationship with the traditional buildings around it.

23

24

ART MARKET
24+25. **The covered market at Arnay-le-Duc, France, by Adelfo Scanarello.** In this setting dominated by stone, the contemporary object plays an active part: the movable sides of this metallic structure – enamelled panels based on the work of English artist Marc Camille Chaimowicz – open upwards like garage doors, leaving the market free to function the way a market should. On non-market days the closed building is a box – but one that rejects muteness in favour of dialogue with its venerable stone surroundings.

25

maze, a totally recyclable musical space made of pine and larch planks that gave off a delicious fragrance when it rained. Here the material is integral to the subject.

Still in the field of sensory architecture, the 1998 masterpiece that is the Kanak Cultural Centre in Nouméa, New Caledonia, is a model of integration with local culture and local landscape. Magnificently set by Renzo Piano between lagoon and ocean, this building was designed as a musical instrument to be played by the antipodean trade winds. A series of wooden shells based on the Melanesian hut, the centre uses its architecture as a sound filter and means of temperature control.

"The huts emit a distinctive kind of noise," says the Genoan architect, who had anthropologist Alban Bensa work on the project with him. "A sound almost that of a voice." Spiking up towards the sky, the tips of the shells dialogue with the New Caledonia pines specially planted to intensify this fusion with the site. And more than ever Alvaro Siza is proved right: "The project is not in your head, it is in the site. You have to look in the outside for the truth of the inside."

27

A PRODUCE CATHEDRAL
26>28. **The Santa Catarina market in Barcelona, by Miralles & Tagliabue**

Above and facing page.
Interior and facade of an idiosyncratic local facility.
The market has been treated as a public space, becoming a covered passageway when not in use.

Preceding double-page spread.
A powerfully expressive structure joyously capped by the coloured ceramic of a projecting, unashamedly undulating roof.

Water and stone, architecture and music come together here in total symbiosis. The architect himself admits that, "I did not expect this simultaneous hardness and softness, this smoothness that was rugged as well, this grey-green iridescence emanating from the blocks of stone. There was a moment when I thought the project had got out of hand, that it had become independent because of a material reality subject to its own laws." That's the magic of the place, you feel like replying.

The sensation generated by a thermal world of this order creates involuntary associations with the work of such contemporary artists as Wolfgang Laib and his wax walls and Giuseppe Penone, with *Respirer l'ombre* (Breathing Shadow, 2000), his tectonic and olfactive space built from bay leaves.

A carpenter turned architect, Peter Zumthor went along with the "installation" game in the Swiss pavilion at Expo 2000 in Hanover. For this celebration of sustainable development he designed an open-air wooden

Covering your tracks

Renzo Piano's "multi-shell" building is confirmation that the identity of a building is no longer as clear as it once was. Its form, like its facades, can express things far removed from its function. So the idea of typology goes straight down the tube.

Who, for example, would ever guess that there was a winery under the handsome stone mantle of the Dominus Estate in California? Delicately permeable to light – and a perfect refuge for the snakes who, legend has it, delight in curling up among the stones – this monolith is the work of Herzog & de Meuron (1998). These apologists for sensitive rationalism put their money on the aesthetics of the gabion: a way of combining the ancestral and the sophisticated, but above all of expressing the idea, crucial in winemaking, of the nature of the soil.

Similarly, who would have imagined the courthouse, at the very least atypical, that surfaced one fine 1999 day in Bordeaux, on the fringe of the old town. Richard Rogers offered the city a baroque monument based on the bottle rack, with courtrooms shaped like demijohns... wooden alembics brought together in a glass box.

Its highly symbolic character makes the courthouse an interesting case. A fragmented

28

ALL SAILS SET
29. The new Fiera di Milano, by Massimiliano Fuksas.
This large-scale project is a pointer to the new generation
of public spaces: more than just a shopping arcade,
the building marks the reinvention of the street as a
1.5 kilometre glass thoroughfare open to all kinds of traffic.

29

COVERED PASSAGEWAY

30+31. **The new Fiera di Milano, by Massimiliano Fuksas.**
There are two levels: the first floor is for paying visitors
to the Fair, and the second, seven metres above, offers
a protected space for travellers emerging from the metro.
The structure – a transparent "veil" supported by slim
masts – plays on shape and height (the latter varying
from 16 to 23 metres) to create visual events along its
entire length. On this site of 1.4 million square metres,
the street is the interconnection between eight exhibition
halls lit by "volcanic" skydomes.

32

SNAKING ALONG THE ASPHALT

32>34. **Noise barrier on the A42 motorway at Utrecht, Holland, by Kaas Osterhuis.** A barrier that stops noise without putting a stop to everything else. This mile long, tapering building is a handsome match with the mobility context it is part of. With its steel frame and glass panelling derived from airplane cockpit aesthetics, it adapts to the speed of passing traffic in intriguing play with the notions of compression and dilation. Utilitarian but not uniform, this hybrid also houses a shopping mall.

structure is also to be found in Salerno, Italy, where David Chipperfield came up with a non-monolithic building based on the alternation of blocks and garden-courtyards. Then there is the magnificent simplicity to be found in the radical aesthetics of Nantes – a black "total look" in high contrast with the red of the courtrooms – conceived by Jean Nouvel as a tribute to Mies van der Rohe. In all three cases, it is the very image of the judiciary as institution that has been amended.

Volcanoes and waves

Other significant examples are to be found under the special heading of length. There is, for example, the kilometre-long slab at Corviale in Rome, that XXL utopia of the 70s; or from the 50s, another social housing venture, the undulating slab at Biscione, clinging to the heights of Genoa. But, now so far away from the time of the Weissenhof estate in Stuttgart, of Le Corbusier's Unités Radieuses and Ricardo Bofill's Walden 7, the architecture laboratory has largely moved out of the housing field in search of new horizons: offices, the service sector, leisure facilities. Whether it's an exhibition site, a company headquarters or something as utilitarian as a noise barrier on a motorway, the responses are strong and specific.

The new Fiera di Milano exhibition centre in Italy (2005) looks much further afield in terms of references than most of its equivalents. Here we have volcanoes and waves up to 26 metres high. Covering a total of two million square metres, the project had to provide a landscape of its own against the distant backdrop of the Alps. The necessary exhibition halls are there of course, but a distinctive approach has interconnected them along a 1.5 kilometre axis that provides the backbone of a lively ensemble. What Massimiliano Fuksas offers is an organically inflected take on Archigram's Plug-In City and the famous Galeria Victor Emmanuel shopping arcade in Milan. Seven metres above ground level, this contemporary glassed-in street is in itself a kind of cinema location, a screenplay full of sequences alternating compression and dilation, an architectural tracking shot conducive to ongoing movement. All the rest is done with the use of orange in an interplay of reflections and vibrations.

Let's linger just a moment in Italy, which, after decades as a stick-in-the-mud, has greeted the new century by opening its arms to modernity: Turin, Naples, Rome – and Stez-

33

zano. There on the autostrada between Venice and Vicenza, Jean Nouvel has imagined the headquarters of brake-parts manufacturer Brembo (project 2002) catching the eye with its "red kilometre", an aesthetically pleasing noise barrier that creates an interface between the motorway and the workaday world. This is a Janus-like building, with two faces looking in two directions and two distinct moods: one facade is a stage set, the other is a backstage, presenting the company as a service industry campus integrated into a natural setting.

Motorways inspire at the moment. See Kaas Osterhuis' project for a noise barrier on the Utrecht-Holland motorway: 1.5 kilometres long and with a built-in shopping mall, it looks like a snake that has just snacked on a rat.

34

The vanishing game

"I want to erase architecture. That's what I've always wanted to do and I'm not likely to

35

WATER AS A BUILDING MATERIAL
35+36. **The Blur: an installation by Diller and Scofidio for Expo 02 at Yverdon, Switzerland.** The "Cloud" produced by water evaporating from the surface of the lake plays on the ambiguity of the virtuality/reality binome. Over a hundred metres long, this ephemeral, totally new environmental and sensory experience was part of the "Arteplage" concept and a spectacle in its own right at the Swiss national exhibition. Moving with the wind, it is not so much an architecture as a host of different architectures.

36

WHERE'S THE FURNITURE?

37. **"Home Palace": apartment in Peking by Didier Faustino of the Bureau des Mésarchitectures.** At the instigation of Diana Cheng, a private developer marked the Chinese capital's first architecture biennial by entrusting a tower block to selected architects and designers. The basic idea: a concept for each apartment. Didier Faustino, whose thing is putting the body "in danger", came up with this two-part arrangement: an outer box of monkish austerity surrounding a core area where the "furniture" is hanging straps you adapt to whatever pose you feel like.

37

change my mind." Thus spoke Kengo Kuma, Japanese designer of the Kiro San Observatory (1994) and a canal museum (1999). The observatory can be summed up as a cut made into a levelled-off hill that the architect set about remodelling. The canal museum, too, disappears beneath a tumulus.

As far as chameleon architecture goes, the footbridge in the forest at Boudry in Switzerland (2003) is a fine display of sensitivity by Genisnasca & Delefortrie and a great demonstration of environmental fusion: wood and nothing but. A kind of branch effect.

The urge to "do" architecture in the landscape without disturbing it and looking intrusive is the driving force for projects that are often manifestoes as well. Future Systems architects Jan Kaplicky and Amanda Levete (organic architecture specialists) have covered their tracks nicely in the "fusion-disappearance" exercise of the Marshall-Andrews house in Wales (1994). This glass bunker embedded in the cliff face is a kind of Cyclop's eye looking out onto the sea, its architecture at one with nature almost to the point of invisibility.

Scrambling perception while clarifying your position is the agenda in France for architects as different as Dominique Perrault and François Roche. Perrault's Applix plant on the outskirts of Nantes (1999) is one answer to the tricky question of the fit between industry and the countryside: a kilometre of stainless steel illustrating the art of the wrinkled envelope. And the disappearing act? It is neatly achieved via the way the landscape vibrates visibly in the architecture. Just a metal curtain that infiltrates the building into the curtain of trees.

Different but just as radical is the "furtive house" concept developed by François Roche (R&Sie), whose Barak house at Saumières in the south of France is the outcome of a novel approach to getting a building permit in a protected zone. The architect has used a textile wall to camouflage his accumulation of concrete blocks, with the area between the two facades becoming a bonus living space.

For Shigeru Ban, textile rhymes with mobile. His Curtain Wall House in Tokyo (1995) cultivates another kind of ambiguity. By blurring its physical limits, the Japanese architect creates an intriguing relationship between the interior of the house and the urban world outside. Large tent-fabric curtains can close off (or leave open) the two-storey veranda of this highly photogenic corner building. The result is first and foremost a concept.

Contemporary architecture is feeding off these multiple ambiguities, and the trend is gaining ground. Thirty years after Roberto Venturi's cult book *Complexity and Contradiction in Architecture* comes The Blur, the star turn at Switzerland's Expo 02 in Yverdon-les-Bains. The work of New Yorkers Diller & Scofidio, this "cloud" – 100 metres wide, 20 metres high, 60 metres deep, hovering over Lake Neuchâtel – was the acme of ambiguity, the zenith of informality, a complete break with all notions of heroic architecture. A hair's breadth from the impalpable, it also suggested interesting parallels with Japanese artist Sugitomo and his deliberately blurred black and white photos of architecture, in which the outline of the Twin Towers or of Le Corbusier's chapel at Ronchamp is enough on its own to generate emotion and a sense of mystery.

Following the American duo's niftily designed scenario, visitors had to enter the cloud wearing sky-blue capes. The cloud itself was in a state of permanent change and amid its proliferation of architectures there was no fixed idea to be had of it. Inside its moist gauziness all notion of perspective vanished, to be replaced by sensory experience – higher air density, lower temperature – and the poetic adventure of a mobile space. The illusion came not from the kind of spatial scenography

38

STEEL LACEWORK

38. **Pavilion in Bruges, Belgium, by Toyo Ito.** European Cultural Capital in 2003, the heritage city of Bruges decided to mark the occasion with two contemporary objects: one permanent – the auditorium by Robbrecht and Daem – and the other ephemeral: a pavilion right in the heart of the old town. Here in the "Venice of the North" the temporary becomes a field for experimentation, with the building's steel lacework set on a specially created pond. It provides both a covered passageway for the public and a space for the occasional art exhibition.

39

40

SPACE SCULPTURE
39+40. **"Syn Chron": installation by Lin at the Neue Nationalgalerie in Berlin, March 2005.** In the Mies van der Rohe temple, Finn Geipel and Giulia Andi (along with Cartsen Nicolai and Werner Soebek) offered a spatial, sensory experience. This multifaceted "light, sound and architecture sculpture" measures 10 x 6 metres, with metal members holding its translucent skin of honeycomb epoxy resin. The inside works both as soundbox and projection area, the sound being generated by "exciters" set on the outside of the membrane and the light projected by laser beams.

once so skilfully used by Palladio in his Teatro Olimpico in Vicenza, but from the ambiguity of the space itself. "Ambiguity is an asset," as Jorge Luis Borges put it. In this enormous "laboratory" exhibition, Swiss artist Pipilotti Rist's "Arteplage" concept, the cloud – an environmental experience if ever there was one – hinged on vaporisation of the water of the lake: 32,000 ducts with 300,000 litres pumped through them every hour. The result was an architecture comprising virtually a single material: water. For the rest, this Blur building harked back to a structure imagined by Buckminster Fuller, inventor of the geodesic dome, but never actually built.

Manifesto installations

Interestingly the same Expo O2 saw Jean Nouvel create his own big event with a monumental, pre-rusted, floating cube on Lake Morat, making 2002 a year of a splendid contrast/complementarity, of two major approaches to the current debate – the immaterial and the sculptural. But looking beyond this endless oscillation between materiality and dematerialisation, the issue was clearly the difference between the conceptual and the plastic.

Notwithstanding its ephemerality, the Diller & Scofidio contribution was a manifesto. The cloud simultaneously embodied hybridization of forms, fusion with landscape and the notion of suspension. "We wanted to create a special effect on an experimental scale," Elizabeth Diller summed up. "An ambiguous space playing on indefinable limits, a hypersensitive space."

In the same year the Swiss pavilion at the Venice Architecture Biennale housed an installation by Decosterd & Rahm intended as a sensory experience both blinding (intense lighting) and chilling (oxygen levels reduced to high-altitude levels). This Hormonorium was presented as the forerunner of a new indoor public space based on the concept of "the disappearance of the physical frontiers between the body and the space." Hyperminimal, Hyperwhite. But like the cloud, it has an urge for ambiguity.

All these installations provide food for thought. As philosopher Peter Sloterdijk has pointed out, the installation, queen of contemporary art, "has little by little supplanted the picture hung on a wall; on offer are not only isolated views and objects, but entire spaces." It means a limitless field for architecture.

Bernard Tschumi and his leaning glass pavilion at Groningen (1990), Dominique Perrault and his glass cabin in Copenhagen (Kolonihaven, 1996), Didier Faustino and his one-square-metre house at the Venice Art Biennale (2002), Zaha Hadid and her tensioned cables at the Villa Médicis in Rome (2000), François Roche and his plastic roof stretched between trees on the banks of the river Baïse in France (Sedimentation, 1996), Stalker's giant hammocks at the Capc museum in Bordeaux (Amacario, 2004), Kaas Osterhuis and his interactive "Muscle" at the Centre Pompidou (2003), Mark Goulthorpe and his choreographically moving structure in Geneva, Toyo Ito and his steel lacework pavilion in the heart of Bruges (2002), French group Periphériques and their pink furniture on place de Furstenberg in Paris: all of them are creating totally new experimental spaces. And we await impatiently 2007 and the major project on the Loire estuary by Jean Blaise, director of Lieu Unique in Nantes, where artists and architects – Daniel Buren, Patrick Bouchain, Duncan Lewis, Kawamata and others – are working on a water-focused itinerary leading from Nantes-Saint Nazaire to the sea. Expo 02's Arteplage has been spreading its tentacles.

41

GREENING THE CONTAINER
41+42. **"Shipping landscape": draft version of an installation at Coüeron-sur-Loire, France, 2007, by Philippe Jamet and Duncan Lewis.** Floating containers covered with plants: this is one part of "Estuary: the Transversal Boundary of the Sea", the major project being overseen by Jean Blaise along the river Loire between Nantes and Saint-Nazaire. The architecture is designed to reflect the landscape: "Layers, strata and epidermises whose history has to be consolidated", as Duncan Lewis puts it.

42

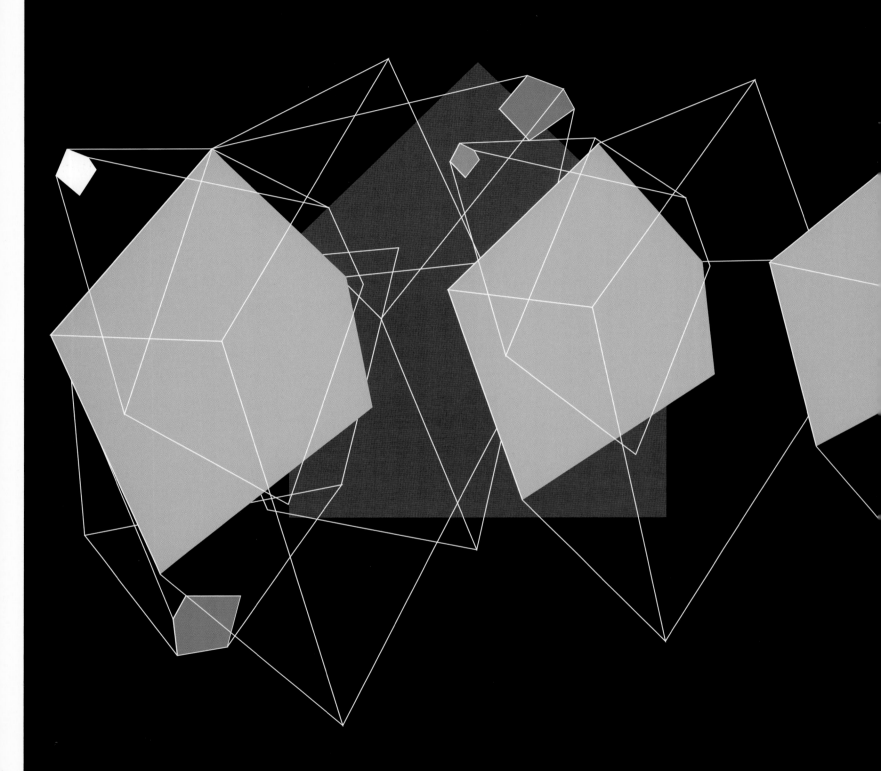

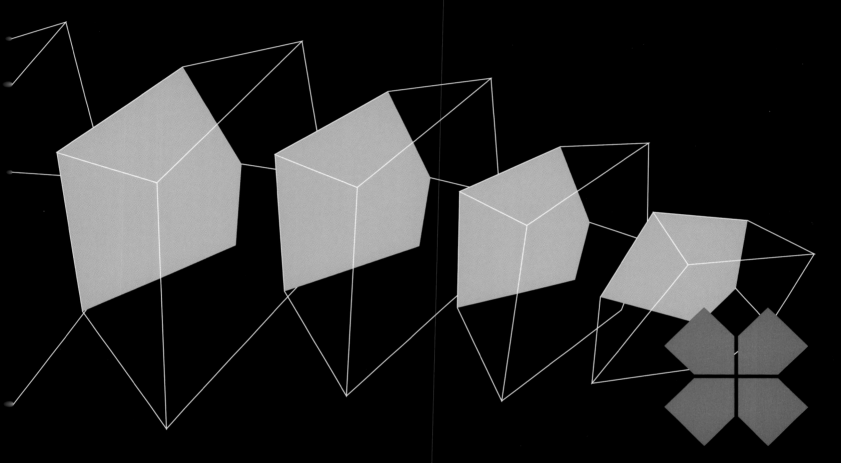

between image and icon

In line with our image-driven society, the city is out looking for points of reference, signals, and symbols. Simultaneously leaving its mark and its landmarks, architecture is putting the emphasis on corporate culture: buildings for fashion, cars, wine – you name it; and the public sector building isn't lagging behind, either. The quest for the contemporary icon is bringing sculptural architecture, a return to geometry and a surge of elusive shapes born of the wave and the cloud.

chapter two

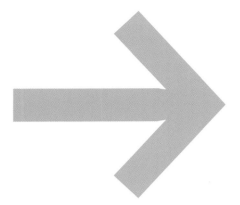

Our image-hungry society is endlessly on the lookout for the icons that succeed each other in the big glossy album of contemporary architecture. But what actually rates as an icon? It's not just such deliciously transient special-event items as Aldo Rossi's Teatro del Mondo, briefly moored at the mouth of the Grand Canal for the 1980 Venice Architecture Biennale; or historic installations like Christo's silver-wrapped Berlin Reichstag in 1995.

With every decade there comes a building that leaves an enduring mark, that stands out in the sense of transcending its value as a chronological marker and attaining the status of a milestone. There are cult buildings the way there are cult films. Tucked away in all our minds are Adalberto Libera's Villa Malaparte as we saw it in Jean-Luc Godard's *Contempt*, and its classical alter ego, Palladio's Villa

1986, when high-tech was king, saw the Hong Kong and Shanghai Bank in Hong Kong. Norman Foster's service industry cathedral grabbed the headlines with its revolutionary use of an atrium as the alternative to the central nucleus approach that was the rule for towers; and artist-photographer Andreas Gursky successfully turned it into one of his minutely detailed works.

In 1997 – the year when Hong Kong historically reverted to China – came the Bilbao Guggenheim. An icon among architectural icons, it had an impact probably as great as the appearance of the Crystal Palace in London in 1851. A century and a half after Paxton's temple to transparency and prefabrication, Frank Gehry's monument revolutionised architecture.

Much more than just a museum, this building, as sculptural as it was contextual – titanium taking over from steel – signalled another generation of projects, another kind of building. Part sea monster, part corolla, the work of the Californian in the Spanish Basque Country stood out clearly from that of his contemporaries. There was something different about it. Tomorrow's architecture was getting ready to spread its wings. In addition to the signal the building represented within the city, it was a sign: a sign of creative flamboyancy and an alternative to banality, an antidote to a globalised, sanitised architecture. This was *auteur* architecture in all its splendour.

Jeff Koons' giant floral dog, mounting guard outside this new cultural temple, was just what was needed for an urban monument that had got the better of a violently intrusive flyover in the heart of the city. The Bilbao Guggenheim spotlights the magnetic power of architecture, offering a symbol of the spectacular restructuring of a metropolis suffering from industrial decline-induced depression. Bilbao, victim as much of industrial change as of terrorism, turned over a new leaf, as it needed to.

43

ICONS FOR THE END OF A CENTURY
43. The Guggenheim Museum in Bilbao, Spain, by Frank O. Gehry. The overlapping volumes of an emblematic building in the heart of Bilbao: an immense, titanium-clad metal structure that had no qualms about including an enormous motorway flyover in its dynamic.

44. The Jean-Marie Tjibaou Kanak Cultural Centre in Noumea, New Caledonia, by Renzo Piano. The ocean on one side, the lagoon on the other: a series of wooden shells inspired by indigenous Melanesian houses, towering alongside New Caledonia pines.

Rotonda, used by Losey in *Don Giovanni*.

The film that mostly deserves our attention here is the architectural newsreel of the last four decades. In 1966 Jörn Utzon's Sydney Opera House, with its white sails swelling above the sea, made its entry via the concert of a modernity liberated from the ideology of the Modern Movement. Then in 1977, in Paris, youngsters Piano and Rogers dropped their anticonformist bomb in the form of the Centre Pompidou, throwing open new horizons on the cultural consumption front.

From landmarks to comebacks
It is time to put things back into context. 1997 saw the simultaneous appearance of the Getty Center, Richard Meier's Acropolis on the Pacific, clinging to an outcrop in Los Angeles; the Beyeler Foundation, Renzo Piano's tribute to "luxury, calm and sensual delight", poised between Basel and the surrounding countryside; and the Kunsthaus at Bregenz in Austria, an "ice cube" of translu-

44

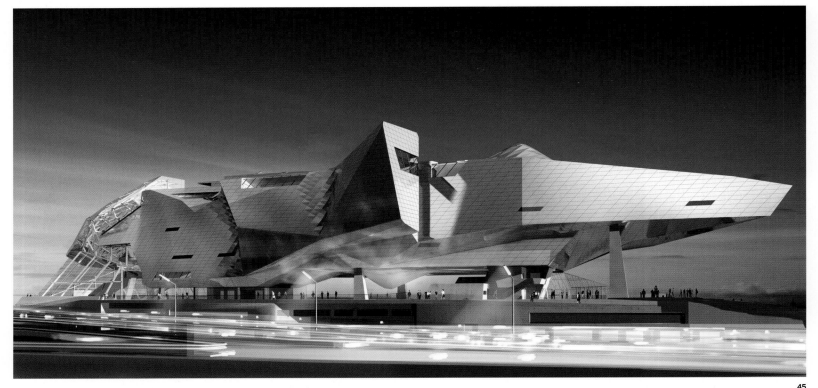

45

THE BILBAO EFFECT
45. **The future Confluence Museum in Lyon, France,
by Coop Himmelb(l)au.** Set between the Rhône and Saône
rivers, the "cloud" at the southern entry to Lyon is
intended as a drawcard for the hitherto neglected tip of
the city's peninsula. Born of morphing and hybridization,
this organic museum-cum-leisure complex is an invitation
to learning and discovery. The giant cloud sets out to
suggest lightness, while a public square slopes through
its accumulated volumes.

cent glass by Peter Zumthor. A vintage year, 1997, with four art shrines – four works, four vocabularies – and to top it all the Gehry Guggenheim putting the avant-garde seal on the end of the century. If, that is, "avant-garde" still has a meaning today…

And speaking of icons, there are also some that never got further than the drawing board, but stick in the mind and ask only to be resurrected. Three mythical projects come to the fore here, each of them with its own diabolically radical idea: the idea of transparency and immateriality embodied by Mies van der Rohe's Friedrichstrasse building for Berlin in 1921, five years ahead of the cult film *Metropolis*; the idea of suspension and urban sculpture in Russian Constructivist El Lissitsky's "horizontal skyscraper" or "Cloud Stirrup", designed for Moscow in 1923; and the idea of dynamics and networking symbolised by Walking City, from Archigram's Ron Herron in 1964.

In one form or another, these three notions turn up over and over again in contemporary architecture. There have been endless experiments with immaterial skins and spectacular cantilevers, not to mention the network metaphor. "There are three kinds of architects," Austrian architect Frederick Kiesler once confided to French art critic Michel Ragon. "Those who have the ideas a long time in advance, so that the second lot can adapt them; and the third lot who are just reactionaries." Today, with the new tools that are available, words like "remix" and "sampling" come more easily. But the important thing is to pay tribute to these architects who have allowed others to convert their touchdowns.

A new feature is the way the icon has become a communication tool. As architecture stars dash around the globe for big-competition face-offs – Yokohama, Los Angeles, Marseille – cities are competing on another, regional as well as international draughtboard. More than ever this is the era of thinking global, acting local. Our metropolises have assimilated the marketing of architecture perfectly, with the necessary attributes as laid down by the English-speaking confraternity: city branding – the city as product; and landmark architecture – architecture tagged as remarkable and even as instant historical monument.

The situation might not be new, but it has become much more marked. Take for example the project for a tower at Hérouville Saint-Clair that hit the headlines in 1988. This extremely European – and never built – *cadavre exquis* bore the signatures, at the

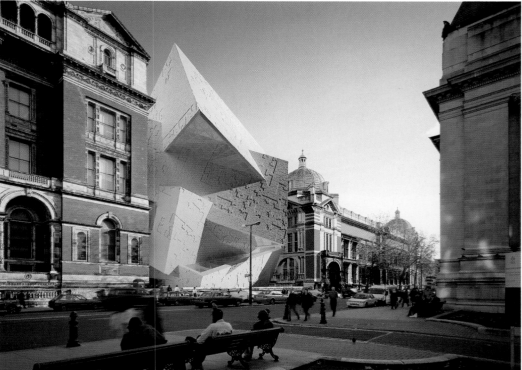

46

time, of the Englishman William Alsop, the Italian Massimiliano Fuksas, the German Otto Steidle, and the Frenchman Jean Nouvel. The then mayor of Hérouville Saint-Clair, a satellite town of Caen, was looking for an urban identity symbol. Never had a building drawn so much media attention and such worldwide praise from the critics; and since then the "Bilbao syndrome" has only boosted the phenomenon.

For some, harking back to the Situationist Guy Debord, this is indicative of an "architecture of spectacle". There is now no shortage of cities out looking for their flagship building, their "Bilbao", starting with Beijing, which launched its National Opera House competi-

RUBBING HERITAGE THE WRONG WAY?
46. **"The Spiral": proposed extension to the Victoria and Albert Museum in London, by Daniel Libeskind.** Dating from 1996 – but since abandoned for reasons of cost – this building was intended as London's newest cultural landmark. With the engineering contribution coming from Cecil Balmond, its marriage of geometry and volumetry is in stark contrast with the Victorian buildings it was supposed to fit with. Entirely coated with ceramic, it uses the interplay of cantilevers and overlapping volumes in a new kind of spatial experiment.

47

GEOMETRY OF THE PUBLIC SPACE

47+48. **The new Marinsky theatre in Saint Petersburg, Russia, by Dominique Perrault.** In its gilt envelope, this 52-metre-high building makes no secret of its openwork power. The intention is full-time contact with the city: the envelope containing a 2,000-seat auditorium creates an enormous covered public space, the sheer volume enabling liaison between all sections of this cultural facility. The smooth aluminium and glass outside of the structure is the opposite of the furious plaster relief-work of the interior. Plus triple glazing as a response to the temperature variations of a continental climate.

48

49+50. The Agbar Tower in Barcelona, Spain, by Jean Nouvel. Set on the Diagonal, Cerdà's celebrated thoroughfare in Barcelona, this 142-metre building now enjoys the same landmark status as the Sagrada Familia. From an elliptical base the office tower rises out of a pool of water to culminate in a glass nose-cone 34 storeys up. Bitmapped all over, it makes play with colour vibrancy via cunning use of a double skin: behind the glass ventelles – translucency giving way to transparence at window level – is a concrete shell coated with a coloured metallic membrane. All in all the structure has 4,400 randomly placed windows, each framed with reflective stainless steel whose interplay of indirect reflections provides unexpected views of the city and the sea.

49

tion in the same autumn that the Guggenheim opened in the Basque Country. And the result, in China, is Paul Andreu's ellipsoidal titanium bubble poised over the water opposite the Forbidden City and due to open in 2006.

Whatever the setting – heritage site or brownfield – the "object" rationale is being confirmed: Dominique Perrault's Marinsky Theatre, a prismatic silhouette due to rise in the heart of Saint Petersburg; the amazing "cloud" of the Coop Himmelb(l)au Confluence Museum at the junction of the Rhône and the Saône rivers in Lyon; the Casa de Musica, the Rem Koolhaas monolith on a square in Porto (2005); and Zaha Hadid's commanding Science Centre in Wolfsburg, Germany, set beside buildings by Aalto and Scharoun. Nor should we forget Renzo Piano's "Bigo" (2001), that flamboyantly monumental marker in the port of Genoa; or the Erasmus bridge in Rotterdam, a proud UN Studio silhouette (1996), which proclaims the reappropriation of the Dutch city's southern sector.

The tendency is such that there are already intimations of a backlash aimed at curbing the impact of the "architecture object". We should not discount, either, the emergence of an altermondialist current, a sort of architectural Porto Alegre refusing to go along with a Bilbao seen as the Davos of modernity.

Political determination

The point is that all these highly newsworthy buildings fit into a city marketing strategy in which political ambition plays a part, with all the undesirable effects this implies. No one has forgotten the tragic error of the Opéra Bastille in Paris, the outcome of a memorable misunderstanding: we were expecting Richard Meier and we got Carlos Ott.

In Europe, city marketing has found itself various venues. In Italy Salerno, next-door to Naples, is using big names to back its architectural policy: Kazuyo Sejima, David Chipperfield, and Zaha Hadid, with one of her cult objects. In Luxembourg, the Kirchberg Plateau has become a star-packed stage: Portzamparc (Philharmonia), Pei (museum), Meier (Hypobank HQ), Perrault (European Court of Justice extension), Vasconi (Chamber of Commerce) and others.

It's the same story at Düsseldorf's river port, where a city very receptive to contemporary art has brought together works by Gehry (an office block-sculpture), Alsop, Chipperfield, Maki, Vasconi et al.

Even Barcelona, with its distinctive standing as a town-planning mecca (thank you, Ildefons Cerdà), is going down the same road. Twelve years after the high point of the 1992 Olympics, the Catalonian capital has big names – Nouvel, Rogers, Perrault, Herzog &

de Meuron – working there, a bit the way Spanish soccer clubs accumulate star players. In the wake of Norman Foster's suspended tower (1992), Jean Nouvel's Agbar Tower (2005), which draws both on Gaudi and the geological landscape of Montserrat, is already the city's new icon. Just like Foster's "Gherkin" in the City of London, except that the Nouvel version openly vaunts its Catalan roots: Foster's tower could be exported to Singapore or Hamburg or… anywhere.

Guadalajara in Mexico is symptomatic of the cinema-style casting rationale, with current stars including Nouvel, Coop Himmelb(l)au, Koolhaas and Ito. And before sinking into the monetary mire, Buenos Aires set out to speed up renovation of the Puerto Madeiro docks with a Santiago Calatrava mobile footbridge; and was betting on Philippe Starck for a new housing concept.

Yet another icon: the Tower of Freedom Daniel Libeskind is going to raise on the World Trade Center site in New York is 1,776 feet tall, to symbolise the date of the American Constitution. This is reminiscent of the Crystal Palace in London, whose length – 1,851 feet – marked the year of its creation, smack in the middle of the 19th century.

Buildings, then, have become a medium in their own right. My focus here is not on the media buildings in Times Square or

52

53

54

WHEN RETAILING BREAKS OUT OF ITS BOX
51>54. **Selfridges in Birmingham, England, by Future Systems.** Highly organic architecture for the driving force of an immense city centre shopping complex. Inspired by the Paco Rabanne dress, the double-skin facade combines concrete with 15,000 aluminium discs. Inside, the spaces are distributed around a vast, skylit atrium, and the mise en scène is emphasised by monumental escalators wrapped in a white plastic membrane. A snakelike footbridge crosses the street, linking the store to its parking lot.

55

BUBBLING OVER

55+56. **The Nardini Centre at Bassano del Grappa, Italy, by Massimiliano Fuksas.** Two enormous elongated bubbles that seem suspended over a pond. These experiments with curved glass – 375 panels in all – stand on their own three feet, with one of them partially supported by a sloping elevator linked to an auditorium in the ground: the ride up takes you from darkness to light

Apart from the actual architectural brief – a building to mark the company's 150th anniversary – the big issue was keeping the surrounding trees. Wrapped in protective netting during the building process, the oaks now dialogue with the transparent envelopes of the structures.

58

59

A WOOD CURTAIN

58>60. **The LVMH building in Tokyo, by Kengo Kuma.** Up and down the trendy Omote Sando thoroughfare in the Japanese megalopolis, the luxury marques strive to outdo each other architecturally. Going counter to the concrete and glass of its surroundings, this building takes a contemporary look at old Tokyo, a city made of wood. Beautifully orchestrated by its sun-breakers, the graphic facade is a curtain made of wood. The Soto-style kinetic effect reappears inside, where some areas are divided up by soft partitions of plastic slats.

Preceding double-page spread.
IN THE BIG WHITE CIRCLE

57. **The Museum of Contemporary Art in Japan, by Kazuyo Seijima (Sanaa).** A big white circle in a Japanese city where creativity and heritage conservation go hand in hand. With no front and no rear, this is a building to be looked at from all sides, an urban meeting point with a catalysing mix of public and exhibition spaces that offer the visitor absolute freedom of movement. In addition to the light source along the entire periphery, the museum is lit by four patios, while its 19 exhibition rooms – with heights varying between 4 and 12 metres – all have skylights.

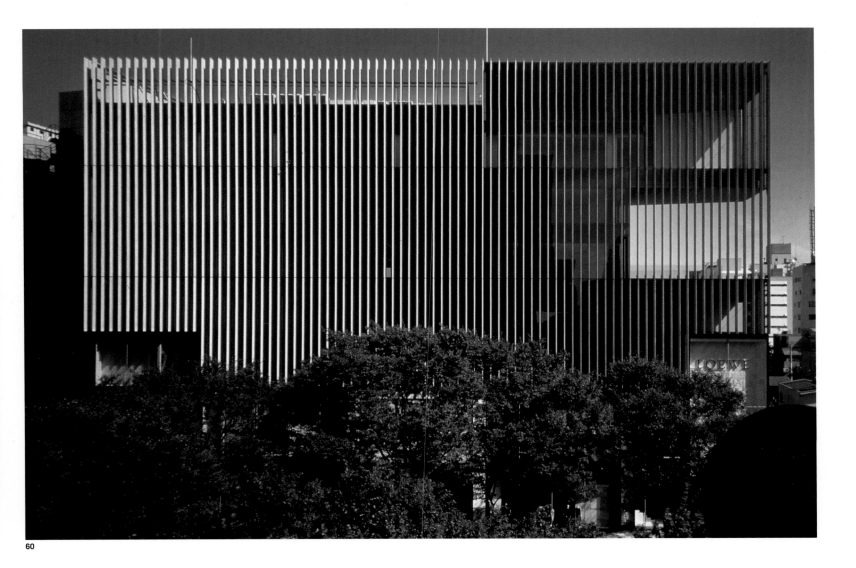

60

TOWER OR TREE?
61. **Tod's Megastore in Tokyo, by Toyo Ito.**
A mix of office and sales space on seven levels.
Under its glass skin the unconcealed concrete frame
symbolises a tree and the building is topped with an
open-air garden. The design is not merely eye-catching:
it optimises the use of the building's open-plan spaces,
while at the same time offering differences of ambience
as you "climb the tree".

Nankin Street in Shanghai, but on a more general phenomenon: the shift from the notion of an urban ensemble – the Versailles of Louis XIV, the Saint Petersburg of Peter the Great, Kubitschek's Brasilia, De Gaulle's new towns around Paris, Pierre Mauroy's Euralille – to that of the object, something more readily usable in communication terms and more readily summed up, or stylised, as a logo. A French example is that what works for the little pyramid at the Louvre (I.M. Pei) also works for the gigantic Millau Viaduct (Norman Foster) and that modern emergence on the volcano scene, the Vulcania theme park in Auvergne (Hans Hollein).

What's more, the tower-object fits this game to perfection. While Paris was timidly renewing its skyscraper debate, London was announcing the highest tower in all of Europe, by Renzo Piano. And in 2004 the Financial Tower in Taipei dethroned the reigning height champion, the Petronas Towers in Kuala Lumpur: 504 metres beats a mere 452. Any more challengers? Yes, Dubai, weighing in soon at 700 metres. Ah, the euphoria of record-breaking!

The Bilbao effect also involves kick-starting the morale of cities that are down in the dumps. The UK example is symptomatic of the new strategies here: before Tate Modern's notorious success in the old Bankside power station, on the south bank of the Thames, the Tate Gallery had already put down roots in Liverpool's dockland, with a dual triumph in terms of culture and new jobs.

So just as in Mark Herman's film *Brassed Off*, in which an unemployed miners' brass band wins through at Covent Garden, a cultural institution has succeeded in reversing a trend; and the host city – like Bilbao – becomes a leisure destination. Similarly in Belgium, not far from the French border, the Grand Hornu mining site is now home to a museum of contemporary art. Totally unexpected in an area eaten away by unemployment, the venture saw architect Pierre Hebbelinck take a sample of 19th-century heritage and add a concrete and black-brick graft. Not far away, the theatre at Valenciennes, in northern France – a red block with well-rounded corners by Emmanuel Blamont and Lou Caroso Neiva (1997) is the lynchpin of a new local planning approach. And now the Louvre in Paris has decided to open an annex at Lens, another former mining town.

Architecture and pulling power

In a period crazy about brand names, an interesting contradiction is provided by the appearance, on the fringes, of a "no logo" architecture. Take, for instance, the petrol station at Houten, on one of Belgium's motorways. Philippe Samyn's highly kinetic enclosure (2001), identifiable only by the large perforated-metal screens that filter both wind and light, gives architecture an eminently specific role. The same spirit is at work on France's A6 motorway, where Bruno Mader similarly sets out to conceal the commercial facets of a rest area, although in this case using wood to produce a relationship with the landscape. This type of project is not at all the same thing as the new, often regionally inflected service villages you see, and the whole new typology of the motorway shopping mall.

And while we're talking about retailing, the surprising new Selfridges store in Birmingham, England – locomotive for a new planning agenda in the city centre – has the distinctive feature of a totally logo-free facade. With its blue skin covered with 15,000 metal discs, reminiscent of a famous Paco Rabane dress, the building is a logo in itself. The pulling power of its architecture (Future Systems, 2003) is all that is needed. "Top of the blob", the *Guardian* newspaper was moved to proclaim when such an atypical building made its appearance in a city that in the early 90s was still an economic disaster area. There can be no denying the "Bilbao effect" of this consumer-drawing machine, a situation propheti-

62

63

64

cally summed up by Andy Warhol's, "One day the shopping malls will be museums and the museums will be shopping malls."

Virtually windowless, Future System's Selfridges uses two atriums to capture light via the roof. Behind the metal envelope of a building designed along the lines of a human body, the public finds itself in a biomorphic universe. The escalators, which this kind of mall cannot do without, are highlighted by being covered with a white plastic skin, the overall effect being one of a fluid space as sculptural as it is sensual. A "snake-walkway" high above the street ensures the link with the car park in the (inevitably) more banal building opposite.

The end of the corporate image

All these high-image, hyperattractive, no-effect-spared buildings play the uniqueness card in urban settings more or less able to cope with them. In the tertiary sector the cult of the icon is part and parcel of the corporate image: tell me where you live and I'll tell you who you are. And here too the trend is towards spotlighting the architectural object: what's at stake is setting yourself apart from the "corporate" architecture whose facelessness helps make all cities look alike.

Since the coming of New York's Chrysler Building – Art Deco with gargoyles – in 1930, a firm's dynamism has often been expressed in points and other sharp edges cutting into the urban space. Recently, however, good corporate health has come to be associated with the image of walking. A delayed-action effect of Walking City? Whatever. After the "ski boot" of Christian de Portzamparc's Crédit Lyonnais Tower in Lille (1994) had stolen a march on the Euralille station, we were treated to Meyer & Van Schooten's "shoe" – the HQ of the Dutch group ING (2003), lording it with its 23 metre cantilever along the motorway just outside Amsterdam.

Harder to get a handle on at first, but equally striking, the offices of the Norddeutsche Landesbank in Germany (Behnisch & Partners, 2002) generate quite a different impression. This totemic 70 metre tower is intended as the anti-monolith, as deconstruction in the interests of the workspace. Paradoxically this deconstructivist metaphor of the vertical city may end up giving the bank in question an image of instability.

In the luxury field, we're looking at a whole other set of referents. More chic, natu-

Preceding pages.
THE CAR CULT
62. **The BMW sales centre in Munich, Germany, by Coop Himmelb(l)au.** Opposite the famous Olympic Stadium and at the foot of the car manufacturer's four-cylinder tower, this home for the "BMW world" is unashamedly spectacular. Beneath the enormous undulating roof are four buildings, one of them an incredibly eye-catching double cone. Buying a car in this playful atmosphere becomes a festive event, and one the architecture celebrates by providing the sales centre with restaurants and boutiques.

63. **The Mercedes Benz Museum in Stuttgart, Germany, by UN Studio.** Not far from the river, but still very close to the motorway, this building uses its spiral shape and interior layout to express a dynamics of movement. The double-helix plan generates two itineraries that intersect over and over, allowing the visitor to change direction along the way. Light comes in vertically via the central atrium that holds the ensemble together, but also through enormous openings orchestrated by slanting columns – a filter that provides a kinetic effect.

Above and facing page.
BONNES VIBRATIONS
64+65. **The Audi concession in Chartres, France, by Berthelier Fichet and Tribouillet.** A symbol of the architectural upgrading of an urban periphery, this group of buildings has been designed to change functions without disfiguring the suburban landscape.
Twin boxes for the staging and a third for the behind-the-scenes stuff: showrooms and workshop, in other words. Carefully calculated architecture gives the ensemble a unitary look: the metal sheeting of the bottom of the boxes is bent upwards to make the roof, and the stainless-steel panels provide nicely shifting vibrations.

65

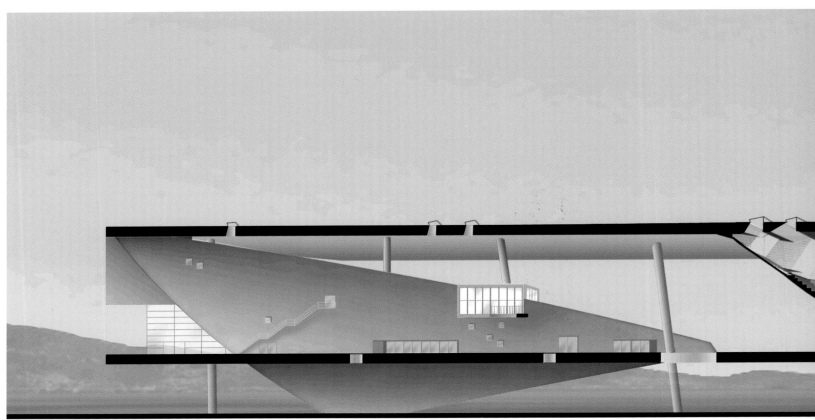

67

THE INS AND OUTS OF INFRASTRUCTURE
67. **The Cidade de la Musica in Rio de Janeiro, by Christian de Portzamparc (currently under construction, opening in 2007).** Volumes in full flight between two broad horizontal planes. Seen here in cross-section the 1,800-seat concert hall can be transformed into a 1,300-seat opera house, with the stage as the sole projection.

Preceding double-page spread.
66. **The Parco della Musica, Rome, by Renzo Piano (2002).** On the site of an ancient villa, surrounded by motorways and only a stone's throw from the famous Nervi sports centre, this new music complex is a series of fragments: three zinc shells – housing three concert halls around an open-air amphitheatre – look like petrified beetles. Each has a different capacity – 2,800, 1,200 and 700 seats – and is wood-lined to look like a musical instrument. A central stage means the orchestra plays surrounded by the audience.

rally. The message here is less the dynamics of form than the sensuality of matter.

Take for example the Tokyo scene, ultimate focus for competition between brands. On Omotesando Avenue, with its succession of top fashion shops, designer architecture really lets itself go.

For Prada (2003), Herzog & de Meuron have run up their glasshouse as a multifaceted diamond. For Dior (2004), Kazuyo Sejima, apparently inspired by the lightness of the French couturier's dresses, has provided undulating acrylic panels which, behind the glass facade, subtly echo the idea of muslin lining. For Tod's (2004), Toyo Ito has opted for an arborescent look. For LVMH (2003), Kengo Kuma's well-proportioned, all-wood facade exemplifies his favourite rhythmics, while on the inside the same serial, kinetic effect emerges from the aluminium-tube walls, the idea once again being to filter light and let the eye rove freely. Also deserving of mention in the megalopolis is the Hermès building (2001) in the lively Ginza district, a distinguished tribute by Renzo Piano to Chareau's Maison de Verre in Paris, but in a context of howlingly bright neon signs.

Across the Atlantic, too, architecture is in there at the heart of the corporate vision. For his LVMH Tower in New York (2000), Christian de Portzamparc also made play with glass, delicately sandblasted this time. But the most striking thing about this building, which was greeted as "jazzy" by the local critics, is its elegant response to the daunting presence of the IBM mastodon across the street. It was out of the question that the black colossus should have its power reflected in the glass of Luxury's number one representative, whence the folds of the facade and a luminous piece of sculpture.

Cultivation of the corporate image can sometimes generate an out-and-out theme park. This is what happened at Weil-am-Rhein, Germany, where Vitra CEO Rolf Fehlbaum has been building a veritable collection of top-architect buildings including a factory by Nick Grimshaw, a warehouse by Alvaro Siza, a fire station by Zaha Hadid, a museum by Frank Gehry and a convention centre by Tadao Ando. Not to mention the Luis Barragan archives, which he has acquired and which will need a home some day.

Since all this helps to animate – or awaken – the city, and make it more attractive, no opportunity is to be missed and no label let slip by: Olympic Games, Universal Exhibition, Football World Cup, European Cultural

69

Capital, the UNESCO World Heritage Listing and so on. Let's not forget how much Genoa owes to its hosting of the G8 Summit. These are the factors that can thrust a city into the limelight fleetingly or permanently: Barcelona has got the syndrome in its blood. And as arguments they feed straight into the theory that Richard Florida, professor of urban economics and analyst of urban attractiveness, outlined in *The Rise of the Creative Class* in 2002. Thus urban development can be seen through quite another prism, with city quality as a leading factor.

Stars of screen and advertising

The Seventh Art adores icons and it will have escaped nobody's attention that one typically hectic James Bond movie, *The World is Not Enough* (1999), includes no less than two emblematic buildings: the Bilbao Guggenheim (yes, again) and London's Millennium Dome, that vast, empty shell put up by Richard Rogers to mark the coming of the year 2000. Quite a milestone when you think that 007's filmography has always put the spotlight on architecture in its most futuristic forms, even carved out of ice when necessary.

A FRESH LOOK AT THE VERANDA
68+69. The Cidade de la Musica in Rio de Janeiro, by Christian de Portzamparc (currently under construction, opening in 2007). Set at the heart of a motorway junction, this is city access with cachet: a monumental cultural signal, a concrete shell floating free of the ground. The idea is to let the beholder's eye rove freely over and through a non-monolithic structure that generously mixes the open and the closed. The terrace-extension of the concert hall/opera house lobby is a truly suspended public space, a vast veranda 200 metres long overlooking a Chacel-designed park of mangroves, lagoons and mango trees.

70

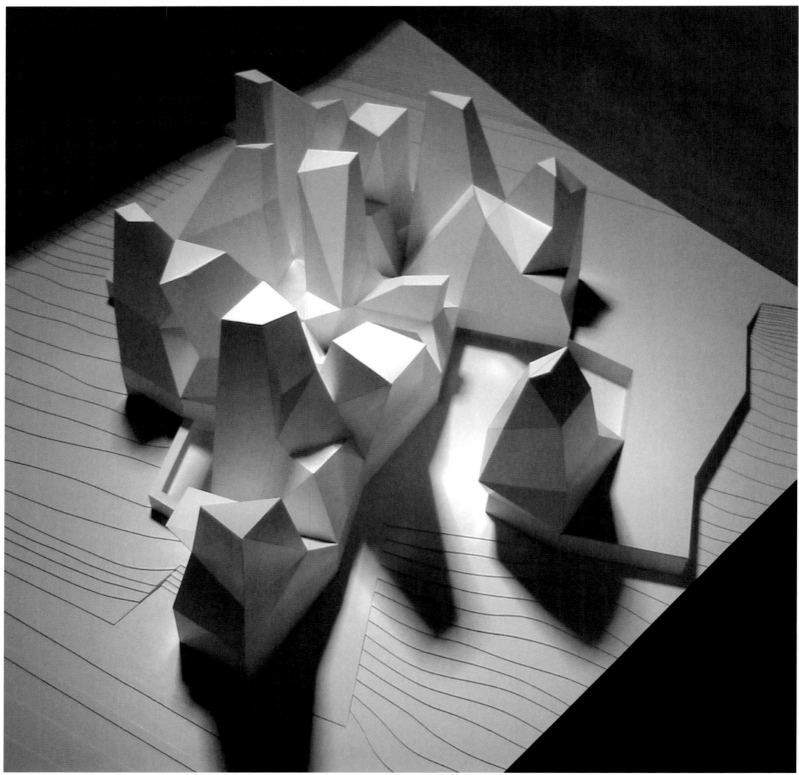

72

Then there are the Petronas towers in Kuala Lumpur, superstars of Jon Amiel's *Entrapment*, with ex-Bond Sean Connery and Catherine Zeta Jones; and Foster's HSBC tower in Hong Kong, transformed into an American Embassy for director Tony Scott's *Spy Games*. True, we're a long way from the magnificently handled urban landscapes of Antonioni's *Profession: Reporter*, Nanni Moretti's *Dear Diary*, and various films by Jim Jarmusch and Wim Wenders. The very same Wenders incorporated Jean Nouvel's "La Tour Sans Fin" ("Endless Tower") project, a quasi-immaterial glass giant set behind the Grande Arche de la Défense in Paris, into *Until the End of the World* (1991) – one way of concretising a building that was never constructed.

Advertising plays the same game in its rapid hijacking of cult buildings: carmakers are the specialists here, urgently chasing architectural references to equate their products with the contemporary city. What happens is a kind of echo effect between handsome buildings and beautiful cars: Mercedes' use of the monumental wing of Calatrava's Lyon-St Exupéry TGV station; Audi's recourse to Zaha Hadid's firehouse at Weil-am-Rhein and Foster's Gherkin in London. Renault borrowed Massimiliano Fuksas and his future Rome "cloud" to sell its vehicles to the Italian market. And the big international car shows are scenes of frantic competition, with Renault employing Franck Hammoutène, and Citroën chosing Christian de Portzamparc, to mention but two.

The car and the city: a couple with its own history. Twenty years after the Renault plant at Swindon in the UK (Foster's yellow Meccano, "Corporate culture" 1983), the most significant strategy is to be found across the Rhine, where automobile manufacturers strive to outdo each other architecturally. Notable are the multiple BMW delivery centre projects – Sauerbruch & Hutton, Coop Himmelb(l)au, Zaha Hadid in Leipzig with a "James Bond" design – and the triple loop of the future Mercedes Museum by UN Studio in Stuttgart.

BROKEN LINES
Preceding pages and facing page.
70+71. **The Cantabrian Museum in Santander, Spain, by Mansilla and Tunon.** This original volumetry is based on a single geometrical unit: the irregular trapezoid. The highly sculptural, geological ensemble links up with the local "fairy chimneys" and the mountainous backdrop. These sky-seeking shapes are designed to capture natural light and draw it down into a museum made up of a whole range of different spaces.

Above
72. **The Toledo staircase, Spain, by Torres & Lapena, 2000.** After making its way over the medieval rampart, the moving staircase heads off in a downwards zigzag cut into the rockface: a zigzag designed in nine sections to cope with the topography and the potentially dizzying steepness of a 36 metre change of level. In this very tricky operation the use of ochre-tinted concrete offers a smooth transition between the similarly coloured upper and lower parts of the city. For the tourists in the 400 buses parked at the city gates, this is an initiatory voyage before they plunge into the old town. And at night the cut made by the staircase becomes a light-filled canyon.

FOLIATION
73. **Apartment building, Rue Pelleport, Paris, by Frédéric Borel.** Clinging to its sloping site in Belleville, this is *auteur* architecture applied to a small plot, a veritable urban sculpture of soaring laminae and coloured concrete. Plus it offers the residents of the ten apartments very special views of the French capital.

After entrusting the wind tunnel to Renzo Piano, Ferrari chose Fuksas for the design centre (2004) on its mythical site at Maranello: a building that plays with suspended volumes, water and colour. For Maserati, Ron Arad swept the sports cars into the movement of the enormous blue ellipse that dynamises the manufacturer's exhibition centre in Modena (2004). Yet advertising, sometimes so skilled in spotlighting architecture, can also kill it. As a moving spirit in the city, with its billboards and luminous displays, it can completely crush buildings – the Maison de Iran in Paris, the Sony Building in Casablanca – and even wipe the city itself off the map at night, when all you can see are giant neon signs; the urban skyline no longer depends on the silhouettes of the buildings, but on the contours of these XXL advertisements. Only a few architects like Shin Takamatsu, with his Kirin Tower in Osaka, have managed to control this chronic overkill.

The sculpture trend

Like artist Richard Serra's *Torqued Ellipses* – enormous, inclined curves of Corten steel sheet that are architectures themselves in the way they define a space between two layers of matter – the Bilbao Guggenheim asserts its status as urban sculpture. The trend it illustrates is not about to go away, to judge by the objects currently being acclaimed in our con-

temporary landscape. Hans Hollein's collages and photomontages of the 60s, showing monoliths suspended over Vienna or aircraft carriers run aground in the countryside, nicely prefigured the phenomenon.

It is clear that today's architect likes to model, sculpt, put things under tension, or in suspension or even in levitation. Thus the questions of aesthetics and of the dynamics of the constructed object mingle in an architectural output seeking to both capture light and captivate the eye.

Daniel Libeskind's bold (but unbuilt) 1998 extension to the Victoria & Albert Museum in London is emblematic of this tendency. On a complex, highly constraining site devoted to heritage preservation, a skilful geometry of triangles, designed on the spiral principal in collaboration with engineer Cecil Balmond, sets out to generate new spatial sensations. In the same architect's Jewish Museum in Berlin (1999), we note that behind the blued zinc facades, with their highly distinctive geometrical openings, the aim is as much a (destabilising) spatial experience as an exercise in memory.

Christian de Portzamparc is overtly a sculptor of urban space. His first work, the Marne-la-Vallée water tower (1974) was a sculpture that could be covered with plant life. Since then he has produced numerous objects with an urban theme, often dedicated to music. The Cité de la Musique at La Villette

in Paris is a piece of city in itself; in Luxembourg, the Philharmonia concert hall, to be opened in 2006, is an elliptical, kinetic sculpture and a tribute to the artist Soto. Across the Atlantic in Rio de Janeiro, white concrete shells mark the Portzamparc's Cidade de la Musica in an alternation of structure and space. Floating ten metres over a tropical garden, this work is intended as a response to the ambient geography. Set amid the tracery of motorway intersections, it constitutes the cultural gateway to the Brazilian megalopolis, between sea and mountain.

Other white shells – or sails – are to be found in Rome's suburbs, as the identifying signal of the church built by the Vatican for the Jubilee in 2003. Less spectacular than the Rio music complex, this group of three curved concrete screens, skilfully put under tension by Richard Meier, nonetheless fulfils the same function: of attracting the eye, and maybe even the faithful. Not to mention the filtering light between the screens;

The notion of a signal expressed by Barragan & Goeritz's famed coloured towers (1957), which for a time marked the entry to Mexico City, makes this a timeless work. In Paris, for an apartment block clinging to the hillside at Belleville (2000), Frédéric Borel, whose taste for Expressionism, as in his Post Office housing on rue Oberkampf in Paris and Institute for

74

LIKE THE BEADS OF A ROSARY
74+75. **Cesar Portela's cemetery by the sea at La Coruña, in Spain.** Leaving the city and looking out to sea on the Galician coast, you see a succession of granite boxes. Following the topography of Cape Fisterra, they seem to have been placed at random, but in fact no box actually faces its neighbour. They are deep enough to provide protection from wind and rain and are fitted with a bench for those wishing to meditate or pray.

75

CYCLOPS HOUSES
76. Single-family houses in Hilversum, Holland, by Maurice Nio & Remco Arnold (Nio Architekten). What might look like a new version of the strip housing concept is first and foremost a response to size requirements: these houses had to be set along an expressway and the result was a Janus-style project designed to shut out the noise while making the most of the landscape. Like angle-parked lorries waiting to be loaded, these identical houses create their own environment. The family car finds its natural place under the cantilevered living room, itself set over the two bedrooms and opening onto to a small indoor garden.

Local Development in Agen, is well known, uses the same components of sculpture and colour to frame views of the capital. Set alongside enormous, impersonal slabs, this building became the de facto symbol of the neighbourhood. Framing makes its appearance also in Lisbon, where the black house designed by Souto de Moura for film director Manoel de Oliveira is nothing less than a machine for capturing views of the city. Nonetheless, it is interesting to note that the primary aim of the system adopted – two boxes set at an angle – was to cope with a major obstacle in the form of a small tower opposite the house. Deftly imposing a diverging squint on the house, the architect has done away with the intruder.

On the fringes of this *auteur* architecture, the monolith effect is still very present, and as much in city settings as in the open countryside. Facing the mythical Matterhorn in the Swiss Alps, Valerio Olgiati's block of white concrete is on the scale of a large rock. Set at an altitude of 3,100 metres, the Matterhorn Experience building is building as spectacle – with a projection room to present the evolution of this magnificent panorama – but a building that keeps its brutalist side, being neither heated nor insulated. Founded on the principle of the square, it avoids the pitfalls of such a basic approach via a mesh effect on the facade.

For his Kursaal in San Sebastian in the Spanish Basque Country (1999), Rafael Moneo set out to dynamise the shape of two translucent boxes. Standing tilted on the beach, they represent a handsome theatricalisation of objects: these are blocks, like rocks, but capable of taking on a lighter aspect, especially at night, when they shed their mineral force to become contemporary lamps.

Geometry as a source of energy

Without it being at all modish, there are plenty of Spanish projects following this eminently sculptural line. In the classical manner the Jorge Oteiza Museum at Alzuza in Navarra, the work of Francisco Javier Saenz de Oiza (2002), seems intent on sticking close to its content: this is a concrete sculpture for a great Basque sculptor, with light-canons pointing at the sky. More sober is César Portela's cemetery by the sea at Cape Fisterra, also in Spain, with its series of boxes – open cubes – dotted like the beads of a rosary along the coastline, clinging to the slope and looking out to sea.

More unexpected is the Expressionist register adopted for the Mansilla & Tunon project for the Cantabrian museum at Santander (2003). Utterly telluric and directly inspired by the local "fairy chimneys", their architecture generates a unique landscape: "A grouping of similar and dissimilar elements seeking to produce a hidden natural geometry," say the Madrid architects, offering a prospect of networked, irregular trapezoids whose points stand up towards the sky.

On a monumental scale in Barcelona, a potent urban sculpture has taken up residence as part of the panorama on the redeveloped sea front at the end of the prolongation of the Diagonale. A giant photovoltaic screen supported by muscular concrete arms is the crux of the public spaces in the city's new Forum. Tilted at 35°, this work by Torres & Lapeña (2004) is part of a plan for reclamation of no less than 184 hectares of public space along the shore.

The same team can claim credit for a remarkable heritage venture, the Toledo staircase (2000), built to connect two parts of the city, one 36 metres higher than the other. This truly is a creative implementation of the notion of a link. Like the famous Centre Pompidou escalator "caterpillar", the Toledo "zigzag" is a spectacle in itself, but one that generates a remarkable relationship with the city, representing an initiatory path to the Castilian old town. The mechanical staircase has been set into the rock and to take it you have to pass under the ancient city wall. The cut made for it dynamises the site, especially at night, when it becomes a lit-up gorge.

Geometry as a source of energy is also the guiding thread for the Laserare stadium built by Eduardo Arroyo at Barrakaldo in the sub-

76

77

MONOLITH WITH A FLEXIBLE FLOOR
77+78. The Casa de la Musica in Porto (Portugal), by Rem Koolhaas/OMA. Making the most of its nomination as European Cultural Capital in 2001, Porto set out to provide itself with a different kind of musical facility. A polyhedron with clear-cut planes, this concert hall is intended as the opposite of the acoustician's beloved shoebox: a downtown sculpture, a white concrete object grafted onto an enormous traffic circle but capable of generating its own public space with a raised-floor set of shops. This cutaway block astutely succeeds in making its niche in the city.

79

80

STRATA AND STRIPS
79+80. **Housing project in Cordoba, Spain, by Maria Galvez Pérez.** Part of the reclamation of a 20-hectare site along the river Guadalquivir, this project is orchestrated by crisscrossing strips. Breaking with the standard slab after slab image and using cantilevers to minimise ground-level crowding, the housing estate is set in a park that also makes extensive use of water.

Facing page.
FEET IN THE WATER, HEAD IN THE CLOUDS
81. **Apartments at Huizen, Holland, by Neutelings.**
Heads proudly raised, the "Sphinxes" – a row of five apartment blocks – are bent on total immersion in their aquatic setting. Each block comprises fourteen apartments designed for optimal lighting. Like ships ready to sail, they are cladded with sheets of silvered metal.

urbs of Bilbao (2003). Here the leader of the NoMad group transforms a brownfield site into a sports venue as playful in spirit as it visually pleasing. The grandstands, already brought to life by their multicoloured seats, are framed by a gigantic Greek fret structure; and when night falls, this polycarbonate crenellation functions as an enormous lamp, providing the city with a new attraction.

Although very different in style, the Basel stadium remodelled by Herzog & de Meuron (2003) fits into the same strategy of making a sports venue into a truly urban object, with its facades neutral during the day and lit up in colour at night. So sports stadiums, which once thrust their concrete bulk on us, are now wearing a new, more appealing garb. In Basel, this means a suit of lights as on a big store.

This gives an indication of just how architects are striving to bring their buildings to life at night, combining interplay of materials and technology. We should not forget Toyo Ito's little wind tower (1986), another aluminium sculpture, 21 metres high, set on a traffic circle in Yokohama, which is nothing remarkable by day, but really something at night. Also worth mentioning here is the Jean Nouvel/Yann Kersalé extension to Lyon Opera House, whose roof stresses the building's function by sending out red signals.

Speaking of light, it is important to point out how much artists bring to architecture (James Turell, Dan Flavin...). The 34 metre long translucent grid, one of Flavins' work (*Untitled; To you Heiner, with Admiration and Affection*) presented in 2004, after his death, in the east wing of the National gallery in Washington is a brilliant example

Did someone say "sculpture"? Listen to Massimiliano Fuksas: "In architecture it is never form or materials that count, but matter." The creator of the initiatory path – all walls of Indaten steel – in the gaping entrance to the cave at Niaux, in France's Ariège region (1993), is back with an assertively sculptural attitude, in the two glass shells overlooking the Grappa Nardini site in Italy (2004). One of these big, hanging "drops" is linked by a sloping elevator to an auditorium set in the ground. Transparent bubbles are echoing now with bushy topped trees.

Canny cantilevers

We're currently witnessing a dramatisation of objects in the city, with the sculpture trend going hand in hand with a distinct revival of

81

the cantilever – as if the void is becoming more and more tempting. Today's structures are seeking, if not to defy gravity, to get their volumes to take off. Going beyond the alignment, breaking out of the frame is a classic Modernist exercise, but one less concerned with creating form than extending space – or better still, inventing it. Using a series of suspended boxes Hennig Larsen has played with the idea all the way along the interior street of a police academy in Copenhagen (2005).

Much more spectacular is the Coop Himmelb(l)au multiplex in Dresden (Ufa Palast, 1998): an object – in a city razed during World War II – in which the tension between a concrete block and a sculpted glass volume acts as an urban catalyst. Designed as a three-dimensional public space – as both balcony and arcade – this film-showing machine openly assumes its status as place: here the cinema is a pretext for creating links. Since the plot has not been entirely used, what is gained by the cantilever is reinvested in the covered area. Highly cinematographic in both its brief and its spaces, the building shatters all idea of perspective and uses its staircases as a stage: the filmgoer becomes actor.

Another leisure venue, another sculpted block, the multifaceted auditorium of the Casa de Musica in Porto (2005) strives for the same dynamic, acting as an interface between the two worlds of entertainment and the city. Located in the heart of town, this concrete monument conveys all the force of an object that seems to have dropped from the sky and grabbed hold of the earth. Yet this is no windowless polyhedron, offering a gamut of views of Porto. Inside, Koolhaas has sculpted the empty spaces, among them the main concert hall, with its openings onto the city at each end, behind the stage and behind the stepped seating. Here we have a building out to establish contact with its city. No question: this work by Rem Koolhaas exudes the same kind of power as Marcel Breuer's Bergrisch Hall (1961), the dual cantilever building that dominates New York University's University Heights campus, or Parent and Virilio's church of St-Bernadette in Nevers, France (1968).

Much more discreet is the elegantly small Brookes Stacey Randall glass house (2000), a locus of utter repose and contemplation above the Thames. Minimal and transparent almost to the point of nonexistence, this volume seemingly suspended over the water seeks to establish a simple relationship with a poetically natural setting. A veritable hymn to small is beautiful.

BIG CHALLENGES

83. The "Villa Méditerranée" project in Marseille, France, by Stefano Boeri. With its bold 50-metre cantilever rising 16 meters above one of the harbor basins, this creation and exhibition arts centre planned for the port in Marseille will be a stone's throw from Rudi Riciotti's Mucem museum. Next door, and still in the water, a second building containing the rest of the programme includes a 600-seat auditorium.

Facing page.
82. The ski-jump at Innsbruck, Austria, by Zaha Hadid. Hook a bridge into a tower on a slope and you've got a sculpture 40 metres high. In this torsion-extension exercise the structure offers a dynamic addition to the landscape, with a café overlooking the city from up where the action starts.

XXL PIXEL
84. The library of the Ontario College of Art & Design in Toronto, Canada, by William Alsop (with Robbie, Young & Wright). From 27 metres up, this incredible box offers a view over a very mixed local bag of buildings. Looking like a table set for dinner, the box is a metal structure resting on twelve colourfully muscular legs and containing two teaching levels. The pixel effect on the outside generates neat interplay with the window openings.

In another case of aquatic outreach, Jean Nouvel's design for a hotel in Brooklyn (project, 2000) is equally in search of a special relationship with the surrounding landscape. Boldly cantilevered out over the East River, this suspended object that returns to the pilotis concept not far from Brooklyn Bridge is looking for a relationship with the Manhattan skyline – but not only, for while even the least well-placed rooms can catch cunningly reflected images of the city, a glass floor offers an astonishing view of the waters of the river.

The idea of living over a void seems to have become part and parcel of Dutch life. Since Piet Blom set his cubes out on the point at Rotterdam in the 1970s, the geometrical and spatial experiments have just kept on coming. MVRDV, for example, offered a fresh take on the drab slab by exploding the horizontal object into the multiple coloured excrescences of the dynamic Wozoco retirement home (1997). In the same year Adrian Gueuze (West 8) and De Architekten brought the same principle to bear on volumes in Amsterdam's Borneo Sporenburg district, their coloured glass boxes breaking with the monotonous typology of terraced housing. In this scenography of everyday life you even find cars parked on the balconies.

Still in Holland, but in a much more monumental register, Huizen's "Sphinxes" (Neutelings, 2003) look like giant sculptures set in the water. Entirely metal-clad, this atypical ensemble of five apartment blocks cuts free of the slab and tower models to bring a new silhouette to an aquatic setting – and a set of neatly aligned, sphinx-like heads.

In a suppler, more open vein, Maria Galvez Perez's housing project in Cordoba, Spain, suspends its slabs along a two-hectare riverbank site. The plan reveals intersecting constructed lines, the idea being to offer greater density than in the old town. There are shifts of typology, too, which enhance the relationship between the buildings and the landscape.

A different challenge faced Stefano Boeri, winner of the 2004 competition for an artists' residence in Marseille, with a concrete building that dips its feet into the port and whose distinctive feature is a long cantilever out over the water. Implicit here is a promise of shelter for the artists inside, just like for the pleasure craft anchored in the harbour basin outside.

Artists are also going along with the "overhang game" as witnessed by Stefan Eberstadt who created a structure which is in the line with 1960s experimentations of a few architects as Chanéac in France or Haus RuckerCo in Austria. "The RücksackHaus", the @@@@ house is a metal box literally hung to the facade of an former textile factory in Leipzig. The visitor is then invited to experiment a new space lit on all the faces of the cube

The best of British boldness
Zaha Hadid is currently looking like the high priestess of the cantilever. Called on in the context of intermodal transport in Strasbourg, France, the Anglo-Iraqi architect had to come up with a tram stop that was also a work of art. The highly plastic result, which brought her the Mies van der Rohe Prize, was a response to an global brief intended to induce suburbanites to park their cars and take the tram: the building intitially catches the eye via the surrounding area, a graphically treated outdoor car park that seems to rise as it transforms itself into a building, with concrete taking over from asphalt.

In Innsbruck, Austria, the nature of the brief and the site made it logical to work on the slope. The Olympic city's new ski jump (2003) is a monument to movement, Zaha Hadid matching her structure to the discipline and relating it to the city. Set at its topmost point, the restaurant seems on the point of toppling into the void, in a situation as close to flight as you can get.

The same architect found herself with a different set of problems on a site in London: the Architecture Foundation in Southwark, on the bank of the Thames. The dual strategy she developed was a kind of oxymoron, being "simultaneously billboard and chapel", as Foundation director Rowan Moore put it. As part of the reclamation of the Southbank dis-

84

trict, this architectural showcase had to be set close to the immense Tate Modern. The nature of the terrain led the architect to push the building's triangular form to the limit and, like the fire station in Weil-am-Rhein, the Foundation finds expression in a thrusting dynamic, with a monumental cantilevered point that both catches the eye and creates the illusion of a very large building emerging from a relatively exiguous site.

William Alsop's Peckham Library in south London (1999) advances outwards 12 metres above its public space. This corner building plays on its material (preoxydised copper) and on colour (the green of the copper and the palette used on the glass facade) and has become a real drawcard, an encouragement to the public to enter a cultural space. Even so, it looks very tame compared to the "table top" concept Alsop put to work so spectacularly at the Ontario College of Art & Design in Canada: a "suspended table" 26 metres up, above existing buildings. The project was constructed in collaboration with the Canadian team RYW in 2003, and its box set on slanted posts is treated with a pixellisation effect that has made it the campus landmark.

There is a lot more violence – some have commented that this was inherent in the subject – in the Centre for the Documentation of the History of the Third Reich in Nuremberg, Germany (2001). Working within a former Nazi building, the Kongresshalle, Austrian architect Gunther Domenig brought such terrifying audacity to his cantilever that an outright feeling of instability is induced. In Vienna, Domenig produced another powerful cantilever with his T-Center St Marx (2003), which appears to be on the point of taking off.

Elemental considerations

In counterpoint to the sculptural trend, another movement is developing revolving around the notion of blur and elusiveness. Toyo Ito and François Roche are really committing themselves to this path, as others explore it in different ways. At the outer limits of the extreme, the Benjamin Colboc and Manuela Franzen project for a refuge in the Andes doesn't exactly make you think of the cabin in Chaplin's The Gold Rush. Nonetheless, hanging from a vertiginous 80° slope, it seems to thumb its nose at the law of gravity. It was built with modules brought by helicopter and has a very distinctive skin made of fabrics functioning as fog captors.

86

The most desirable form of all at the moment, both as metaphor and, even more so, as application, is to be found in the domain of the wave and the cloud. Of the influence of the elements on architecture, it makes one think of Courbet's famous painting *The Wave* of 1869, with its foaming roller and heaped-up clouds offering their dramatic evocation of movement as idea. But it could be *Pointbreak*, Katryn Bigelow's movie where characters are surfing as well as on air as on sea, or "Teahupoo", this legendary Tahitian wave with 6 metre high curve water screen; And of course the wave concept has already gone global via the Nike swoosh…

Massimiliano Fuksas has worked on the idea in his very own, very radical way in the Candie block, a little quarter tucked away behind the Opéra Bastille in Paris. Starting

UNSTEALABLE VIEWS
86. **Office in Fussach, Austria, by Baumschlager & Eberlé.** A radical concrete sculpture for an unbeatable view of Lake Constance.

Facing page.
85. **Project for a refuge in the Andes, Chile, by Colboc and Franzen.** An interestingly wrapped up, gauzy effect on a building likely to find itself coated with frost.

87

NOTHING LIKE A GOOD READ

87+88. The Médiathèque in Troyes, France, by Lyon and Du Besset. Given that this cultural facility had to compete for people's attention with a fast-food outlet, the architects opted for a shifting, elusive geometry. The attention-getter is a porch roof connecting up with the undulating wave of metal unfurling along the entire length of the reading room. An expanse of gold leaf in a world made of books. Artists played quite a part in shaping this very city-oriented building, among them Lawrence Wiener and Gary Glaser for the colour scheme.

88

CAPTIVE CLOUD
89. **The inside of the future convention centre in Rome, by Massimiliano Fuksas.** In the capital's Eur district, a temple to 1930s modernism and Italian rationalism, this is a building striving for dialogue by using the formal/informal dichotomy to assert its identity. Imprisoned inside its glass box is a large free-floating "cloud". This textile-wrapped metal structure houses the conference rooms, thus freeing up 15,000 square metres of lobby space and generating a dreamlike atmosphere marked by the recurring Fuksas urge to build little cities.

89

90

FLOATING BODY

90. *Marsyas,* **a work by artist Anish Kapoor (2002),
at the Tate Modern, London.** With its three steel rings, each
30 metres in diameter, this work matches the gigantic scale
of the 150-metre long Turbine Hall in the former electricity
plant converted by Herzog et de Meuron. Monumentally
enigmatic, the work is an exercise in mystery that never lets
the beholder grasp it completely. Engineered by Cecil
Balmond, this long steel structure covered with a skin-
coloured membrane – it seems at once intestine and
eardrum – suggests an organic, physical world. "I want to
create a body in the sky," its creator had declared.

91. **The DG Bank headquarters in Berlin, by Frank O. Gehry**
With no hint of its existence on the outside, where the
artist's stone facade politely complies with the "critical
reconstruction" of the Pariser Platz, the structure housing
the boardroom is the big event in the atrium. Between the
glass of the floor and the glass of the ceiling, this space
based on the shape of a horse's head is a model of fluidity
and formal freedom. The shell of this meeting area is
covered with steel on the outside and wood on the inside.
The other surprise here is the skylounge, in the upper part,
with its view of the Brandenburg Gate and the glass dome of
the Reichstag.

with the idea of a fusion of sport and housing
in a very urban ensemble, the Roman architect's scenario comes wrapped in a single
skin: zinc. The result is a very Parisian shell in
the form of a large, well-rounded fold, a totally unexpected wave in the ocean of the capital's roofs.

This wave can sometimes turn out tremen-
dously sculptural, as in the giant curve signi-
fying the presence of Santiago Calatrava's
shoreline auditorium in Tenerife (2004). But
it can go off looking for other formal outlets
too: gentle waves as in the movement of the
roof of the Paul Klee Museum in Basel (Renzo
Piano, 2005); a wave forming a fashion
amphitheatre in the heart of the Prada store
in New York's SoHo district; a wave coursing
across the gilded ceiling of the Médiathèque
in Troyes, France (Lyon & Du Besset, 2002).
Waves can be found in public spaces too:

a suspended wave right in the urban heart
of São Paulo (Praça di Patriarca, by Mendes
da Rocha, 2002), and the ethereal loops
of the one breaking on the new Diagonal Mar
park in Barcelona, designed by Miralles &
Tagliabue (2004).

If you want different kinds of swirls and
eddies, try Michigan's Lake Chicago. Working
with curved pieces of steel, Frank Gehry's
very rock'n'roll project for a concert hall in a
public space gives the impression of waves
rolling in and breaking at the foot of the
imperturbable towers of the Illinois capital.

Meanwhile the clouds are heaping up
before our very eyes. This is an idea that has
really taken off since Peter Rice's stagnant
cloud right there in the empty space of the
Grande Arche de la Défense, hanging from
Spreckelsen's monument. Diller & Scofidio
have already shown their version at Yverdon-
les-Bains, and Coop Himmelb(l)au have
drawn on this celestial register for the forthcoming Confluence Museum in Lyon.

Ideas are often described as being "in the
air". The big flying saucer exhibition at the
Fondation Cartier in Paris in 1998 featured a
Panamarenko structure floating inside Jean
Nouvel's glass building – a fleeting moment
that we will doubtless recapture in 2007 in
Rome, where Fuksas is getting into the theme
on a grand scale: impatience is building around
the "cloud" to be enclosed in the future convention centre in the Eur district, already an
architectural mecca. And just how is this textile structure going to stay in the air?

The cumulus image is a reminder of the
unexpected appearance in 2000 of a series of
bubbles in the rolling Cornish countryside in
southwest England. From the hand of Nicholas
Grimshaw, the biomes of the Eden Project at
Saint Austell show us how geometry, run
through ecological and computer filters (one
of the aims here was to calculate the effect of
sunlight on microclimates) can give rise to a
truly unique place. Starting out with a vision
of nature and backed by engineer Anthony
Hunt, the man who gave you the Eurostar terminal at London's Waterloo Station has come
up with a sort of artificial paradise and a great
contribution to 21st-century botany.

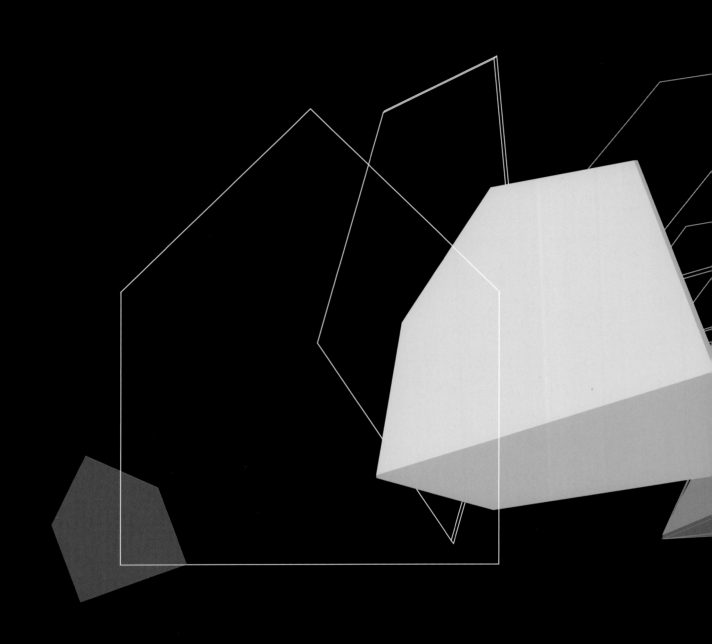

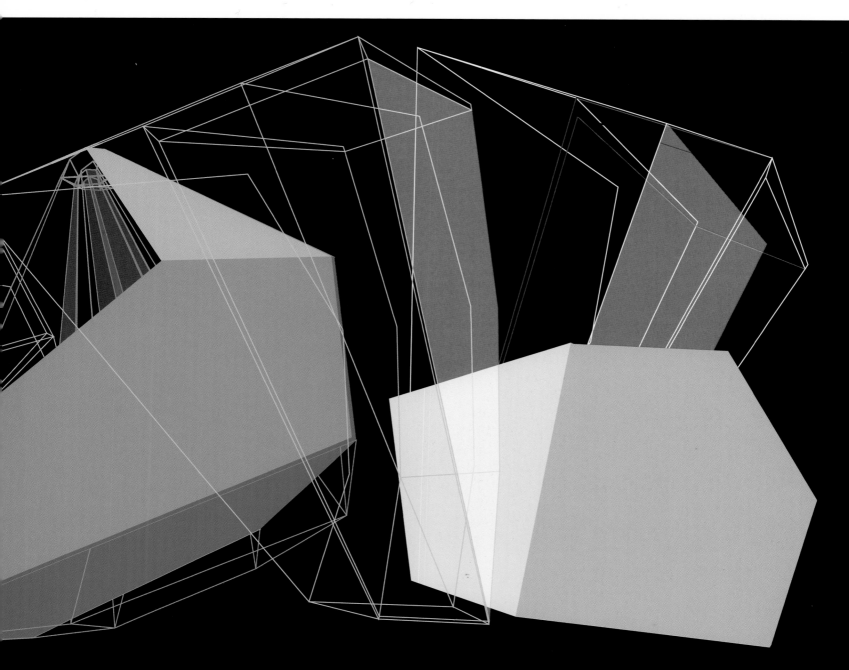

mutation and experimentation

Computers have revolutionised what goes on in architecture studios. Morphing, for example, makes possible thoroughgoing spatial metamorphoses, and experimentations with totally new places and concepts. More organic than ever – all those "blobs" – architecture is now looking for inspiration to the natural world and living systems. Recurring themes are the "fifth facade" and the "continuous surface", with the latter exploring the possibilities of folding and braiding.

chapter three →

92

nals a whole organisation created to separate thinking from realisation. This synergy could be interpreted as a very marketing-oriented approach, but the aim is to prepare concepts, whether they will ultimately be built – or not. Thus when Rem Koolhaas finds himself thinking about an image for an enlarged Europe, he suggests changing the yellow stars on the blue flag to a bar code – 25 bars for 25 nations.

In the 1920s the Russian constructivists, led by Ginzburg, were proclaiming that "The architect is no longer a decorator of life, but an organiser." An organiser with no mean talent as a handyman, for if French thinker Emil Cioran is right, "to be modern is to improvise with the incurable." So now is the moment to act for cross-disciplinary groups of architects, sociologists and artists – Stalker in Rome, the cooperative A 12 in Genoa, Cliostraat in Turin, Cero9 in Madrid, the Armengauds (AWP) in Paris – who work on the everyday experience of architecture, without forgetting the tireless group Site (standing for Sculpture in the Environment) in the United States.

"An architect," said the great French architect Philibert Delorme in the 16th century, "is a builder who can speak Latin." 500 years down the track the architect, if he's not the high-minded artisan the profession still possesses, might very likely be a kind of art director, fluent in digital-speak and relaxedly checking his sites out by webcam. In the age of "starchitects" and globalised work methods, Dutchman Ben Van Berkel puts a point of view derived from working in a highly sophisticated team: "The architect is going to be the chic creator of the future." The mythical architect-artist so superbly embodied by Gary Cooper in King Vidor's *The Fountainhead* (1949) is only a background figure now.

Agencies are changing in scale and strategy. Rem Koolhaas and his OMA team might be really unique, but they are also a revealing example of how the profession has changed. The think-tank-inflected creation of a second unit (AMO) within the agency bespeaks a quest for complementarity, but above and beyond the mirror effect (OMA/AMO), it sig-

The digital revolution

There is a before and after Bilbao. Frank Gehry's Guggenheim was a turning point in more than one sense, a titanium opus that celebrates the triumph of freedom of expression as much as the architect's computer-driven mastery of design. Opening the doors wide to morphing, the digital revolution has brought profound change to architecture's mode of representation.

In 1998 Asymptote – the New York team of Hani Rashid and Lise Anne Couture – computer-produced the first virtual reality space in the form of a virtual stock exchange. Since then, and sticking with computers, Asymptote has provided the complexity and the dynamic lines of the Hydrapier (2003), a multimedia pavilion at Haarlemermeer in Holland: 100 metres long set between the water of the polder and the cascading sheath of water that permanently covers its roof.

Given the steady rate of technological advance, the new millennium is confirming the accelerated growth of the computer gener-

93

BLUE BLOB

92+93. The Kunsthall in Graz, Austria, by Cook and Fournier. Built as part of a series of artistic events celebrating the city as European Cultural Capital in 2004, this is an odd kind of building to find among Graz's onion-domed churches. Like a sea monster washed up in the heart of the old town, the museum is a soft sculpture with no distinction between facade and roof: its swelling body has a single acrylic skin pixellated with 1,000 subcutaneous luminous discs that make it change colour at night.

Following two-page spread.
94. The blob-type building is spiked with nipple-like "chimneys" that shower the interior with light, both artificial (from their neon circles) and natural.

MUTANT MUSEUM
95. **The MU: the winning project for the museum of contemporary art in Bangkok, by François Roche, with Stéphanie Lavaux and Jean Navarro (R&Sie).** With its bones discernible through its metal skin, this is architecture that merges with its environment. Deliberately designed to incorporate the effects of Bangkok's pollution, it changes appearance as time passes, its aluminium mesh cover acting as an electrostatic system. This same outer garment covers randomly combined concrete blocks, the result being a rocky urban outcrop reminiscent of Phang Nga rising out of the sea near Phuket.

ation, with digitalisation going hand in hand with increased conceptualisation. These days plenty of architectural projects are direct products of software manipulation, and on every scale, be it something of the size of the Yokohama ferry terminal (Foreign Office Architects) or a project as small as the 56-square-metre Loewy bookshop in Paris' Marais quarter, with its "lived-in book towers" (Jakob & MacFarlane). Meanwhile, in Naples there's the collaboration between an architect and an artist: Future Systems with Anish Kapoor. Morphing is where it's at.

It could hardly be clearer that information technology, initially much feared by architects, has pulled off the big shift. Yesterday's enemy is today's objective ally, with the computer validating hitherto unthinkable options. But let's be frank, the machine only helped the profession surmount the obstacle of the seemingly unfeasible and do away with doubts as to architecture's potential: traditional practice had already provided forms prefiguring all sorts of innovations. Stretched structures and inflatable structures ranging from spider's webs to soap bubbles signalled a whole new world of metaphor.

Bubbles come in different forms, too – we need only look at Beijing modernity: while Paul Andreu is completing his titanium bubble National Opera House, the PTW team is using the bubble element for the kaleidoscopic facade of the box housing the Olympic pool.

Nonetheless, the dangers of "computer architecture" are very real. Imagine, for example, a film that depended entirely on its special effects and paid no attention to the screenplay. Jean Nouvel's warning merits our attention: "It's easy to copy just by changing a single parameter, without giving any thought to insertion and without there being any invention in the poetic sense. The big danger is cloned or genetically modified architecture."

The fact remains, however, that absolute control of the machines that cut the steel for the vast tracery making up the Bilbao Guggenheim has really boosted architects' – and clients' – confidence, without any loss of materials or of creative power. This time we have the proof that a bold, large-scale project can be brought to fruition without running off the financial rails while – and this is vital – remaining totally faithful to the original design. The budgetary and creative lines can hold, right down to the last millimetre.

The key to the success of Gehry's Guggenheim can be traced back in part to a technology transfer. The museum was worked up like an aeroplane, using the Catia aeronautics software from Dassault Systems. Interestingly Norman Foster – an aeronautics freak if ever there was one – gave an architecture lesson on British television back in the 1990s using a Jumbo 747.

Since Bilbao, Gehry has pursued his experimentation via such major, eminently sculptural cultural ventures as the Experience Music project in Seattle (2000) and the Walt Disney Concert Hall in Los Angeles (2003). This has led him into a partnership with Dassault aimed at developing markets – naturally enough – but above all "projects". And these projects are not necessarily his own: Gaudi's unfinished Sagrada Familia in Barcelona, for example, is going to benefit from the new technology – even if the question still looms as large as ever: does this mystical symphony really have to be finished?

When aliens invade the city

New tools favour the appearance of new and utterly strange forms. Blobs, for example, and the "blox" you get when you put blob and box together. Invading aliens have sneaked into the contemporary city: just look at the boardroom of the DG Bank on Berlin's Pariser Platz, Frank Gehry's morphing of a horse's head (2000). And the invasive presence is highly visible in the water pavilion in Holland, based on a 14-ellipse structure and washed up like a whale on a beach (Nox, 1997). Then there's the Peter Cook/Colin Fournier Kunsthaus in

95

Graz (2003): this soft form covered with "nipples" (skylights for the museum) provides an exciting confrontation in the heart of the old city. The "blue blob" talks back to the onion domes of the churches, its cladding of 1,300 curved acrylic panels metamorphosis at night when the 930 light circles slipped under the biomorphic building's skin come to life. Peter Cook himself describes the object as a "friendly alien", a blue beast that's not there to frighten us.

Treating the environment as a veritable genetic code, François Roche (R&Sie) is producing projects espousing a much more active contextualism. The idea is to create not a form, but an interface between building and environment, between interior and exterior. House or museum, the approach is the same. In Bangkok, though, he offers an ectoplasm. Here strangeness of form is matched only by originality of process: the metallic skin of this museum of contemporary art and design (project, 2002) aspires to change with time. Designed to agglomerate the dust of a dramatically polluted megacity, the active, informal facade is simultaneously rugged and smooth, and points up the complex organisation of the exhibition rooms.

In the same vein of an architecture exclusively conceived of as something living, the glaciology museum at Evolène in Valais, Switzerland (project R&Sie, 2003) also cultivates a certain ambiguity. The object is at once monolithic and spatially complex, and based entirely on the digitalisation of a traditional habitat. But at an altitude of 1,500 metres, according to its architects' scenario, this informal wooden block is very quickly going to become a block of ice. The American Peter Eisenman has resorted to the same genetic code notion to justify the spirit of his cultural complex project for Santiago de Compostela in Spain (2006), neatly deconstructing the scallop shell form so bound in with the ancient symbolism of the place.

Foam and Sponges

Computer tools give architects a marvellously free hand with the organic notions that remain a major theme. Young Madrid architect Andrés Jaque, for example, has used them to ponder other living styles, notably in his project, prepared in association with economists and sociologists, for Stavanger in Norway. Taking into account the changes in our society – mourning, separation, the recomposed

97

family, etc – he works with the idea of the hyperflexible apartment building. From one architectural point of view the project is an immense glass sponge with living cavities. Jaque himself prefers the word "foam" to signal the lightness of a concept entirely devoted to mobility.

The same kind of informality is aimed at by The Sponge, the sadly unbuilt Toyo Ito/Andrea Branzi project for Ghent in Belgium (2003). A remarkable concept and a remarkable way of activating a site's potential and bringing new uses to light, it was quite simply, a sponge to wipe away the notion of partitions and express the fluidity of the spaces: "A very simple building on the outside, but very complex inside," says the Japanese architect. Inspired by biology, the building is approached here as a living organism, and it would have been interesting to see how Ito actually realised these "sound and perceptive structures". Doubtless this kind of project will turn up again somewhere, someday.

The question now is the potential for change of nanotechnology in terms of our everyday environment. Could architecture become reactive, like those sports shoes whose

STACKING AND TANGLING
97. **The Eyebeam project, New York, by Diller and Scofidio.**
For Eyebeam's creators, multimedia means multidimensional. The facade of this Möbius building – a dual vertical strip combining a film of concrete and a film of resin – explains its hybrid function as a venue for artistic creation and exhibition. What the architects have done, in fact, is ignore the issue of the facade, priority going to appropriation by the multimedia artist occupants.

Facing page.
96. **Project for the glaciology museum at Evolène, Switzerland, by François Roche, with Stéphanie Lavaux and Jean Navarro (R&Sie).** This ghostly experiment is the outcome of the digitising of a model of a traditional apartment building. The interior volumes become visible as excavations into the volume, like cavities in a glacier. The end result is overlaid wood shingles – local larch – in a steel wire cage that traps snow and frost in winter.

Preceding double-page spread.

SOUND SPONGE

98. **"The Sponge": unbuilt 2004 project for a municipal auditorium in Ghent, Belgium, by Toyo Ito and Andrea Branzi.** Its designers described this project as "enzymatic". The real surprise is inside: through the glass skin you can make out a spatial complexity running completely counter to the standard concept of the enclosed auditorium. The key here is the sponge, with its transformable cavities. Intended as a living organism, this sensory experiment is remarkable for a spatial fluidity in constant touch with both the city and its river.

FROTH AND BUBBLE

99+100. **The "Froth City" project for Stavanger, Norway, by Andrés Jaque.** Intended to evolve in time with social change, this 2003 residential project puts the emphasis on flexibility and optimal living-together. With its clear Archigram influence, this is an attempt at innovative management based on accommodating shifts within the family. The blob effect is achieved via a proliferation of glass bubbles.

built-in sensors react to the surface underfoot? Time will tell.

Naço, a parisian team which imagined a "Skin house", are among those architects who have experimented in that direction; It's worth noting that the Biowall, a smart partition born of a cross between electronics and biology, made its appearance in the lab at the Lausanne Polytechnic (EPFL) in 2002.

Innovation and invention remain the privilege of a handful of pioneers. Shortage of funds means that agencies have trouble experimenting on the scale they would like to, whence the problem of how to push ahead with research without having to sell your soul to big business: architects can't afford to become sales reps for manufacturers. This explains the option taken by Dominique Perrault, to whom we owe the development of very large-scale metal mesh, as in the Berlin sports complex (1999), the "breathing glass" of the Vénissieux (France) Médiathèque (2001) and the Tenerife hotels (2006): he gets his research done in an ad hoc lab at Zurich university.

Technology transfers

Let's try a brief comparison with a couple of top chefs, Frenchman Pierre Gagnaire and Catalan Ferran Adria ("El Bulli"), both of whom work with chemists. Adria designs, if not to say "constructs", his dishes with liquid nitrogen, experimenting with tastes and combinations via a creative, science-inflected quest for innovation.

Likewise today's architecture is continuously enriched by technology transfers, drawing for instance on boat-building in its creation of new spaces. The metal "bubbles" or "pockets" designed by Jakob & MacFarlane for the restaurant Georges on the 5th floor of the Centre Pompidou reflect this kind of input. As no regular building supplies company could produce the shape in question, the architects went to a racing yacht manufacturer. William Alsop did the same in London in 2003: called on to remodel Victoria House, an Art Deco office block, he had his composite coloured capsules made up in a British shipyard. Jakob & Mac-Farlane also had recourse to aerospace technology – honeycomb panels – for the big folded screens that structure the central area of the Renault Communication Centre at Boulogne-Billancourt (2004). As for François Roche's "furtive" Barak house at Saumières in France, the textile skin is derived from orchid greenhouses; and construction was entrusted not to a builder, but to a freelancer with experience in putting up circus tents.

If there's a flourishing area of experimentation at the moment, it has to be the vegetal, which is really developing on the urban front under pressure from ecologists and local community groups looking for more greenery. Here too we're looking at the "disappearance" of architecture and the "chameleonisation" of buildings: nature as a thoroughgoing architectural material, and even the binding force for a new urbanism. Will the next step be "agritecture"?

Patrick Blanc, architecture's botanist, has shown that you can make just about anything grow on very thin walls. After bringing a giant vegetal composition to the gable wall in the courtyard of Andrée Putman's Pershing Hall hotel in Paris, he provided London with

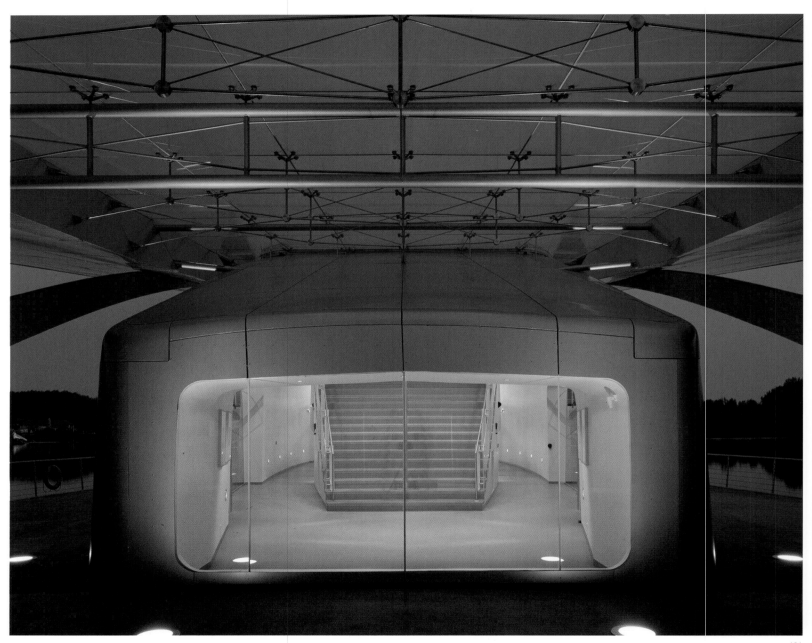

101

BETWEEN EARTH AND WATER
101+102. **The Hydrapier pavilion at Haarlemermeer, Holland, by Hanni Rashid and Lise Anne Couture (Asymptote).** On a polder not far from Schipol airport, this building plays on the registers of earth and water. Tapering like an aeroplane, it draws complementary values from its aquatic setting. Originally designed to house a world horticulture show in 2002, it makes its impact with its linear dynamic. Particularly notable is the surfboard-derived roof, with a glass swimming pool whose water, pumped up from the lake, flows down the walls at the entrance.

102

103

105

VEGETAL ARCHITECTURE

105. The "Flower Tower" apartment block, Paris, by Edouard François. Opposite a garden surrounded by a variety of building styles, this facade catches the eye with its movement: bamboo growing in enormous concrete pots.

Preceding pages.
SAW-TOOTH DYNAMICS

103+104. **The Renault Communication Centre at Boulogne-Billancourt, France, by Jakob & MacFarlane.** A new life for one of the few remaining parts of the old Renault factory. The original was designed by Claude Vasconi in the 1980s, with its assertive saw-tooth roof system offering a regular rise and fall from 6.9 to 12 metres. This time round the architects went for enormous vertical walls with sharp folds, providing maximum flexibility for an exhibition area of 6,000 square metres and tangential views of the enormous central section from the mezzanine. Consummate sleight of hand transforms a huge, opaque wall into a glass curtain that connects the former factory with the extensive urban park now developing around it.

a totally vegetal bus shelter. Back in Paris, Jean Nouvel used Blanc's talents to work up the facades of the Musée des Arts Premiers, in an highly unexpected knitting of the new to the old.

Vegetal architecture is now finding a foothold even in the most urban contexts. After a mobile auditorium based on a genuinely arborescent structure, the Tetrarc group created apartment blocks in Nantes in which each apartment has its own tree; this vertical arboretum now works as a visual filter on the banks of the Loire. Among other "green facade" experiments are Duncan Lewis's lycée at Obernai in Alsace, France, and Edouard François' Flower Tower in Paris: rental accommodation whose facade, made of enormous, bamboo-sprouting concrete pots, actually moves in the wind. Like Adrian Gueuze, who imagined a vegetal tower for New York, Edouard François has also proposed a 70 metre green tower for Brussels.

For a more militant approach, try Sarah Wigglesworth & Jeremy Till's earth and straw "eco-nut" apartments in London (2002). The idea is gaining ground in the Czech Republic, too: in rural Mlada Boleslav in 2003, Peter Suske built a house with facades made of bales of straw and a canvas roof: no insulation problems there.

At Chino, in Japan's Nagano province, the intent is less overtly ideological. In 2004, adopting a stance very much in line with the local culture, Terunobu Fujimori built a tiny house there, a sort of cabin that could have come out of Italo Calvino's *The Baron in the Trees*. All of 6.6 square metres and with no sanitary facilities whatsoever, this teahouse-inspired mini-residence is simultaneously quasi-invisible and easily spotted in its natural setting. Incredibly, given that it is set two metres in the air atop a pair of splayed, stilt-like tree trunks, the house achieves perfect balance. Inside and outside, everything is hand-crafted, from the cob walls to the wood-tiled roof. Architecture plus texture.

At Nova Viçosa, in Brazil's Bahia state, the tree house-cum-studio created by architect Zanine for the sculptor Frans Kracjberg, author of the Negro River Naturalist Manifesto, is also looking for this kind of osmosis. In France, Lacaton and Vassal's Dartois house at Picquey, on the Bassin d'Arcachon (1998), combines the same up-in-the-air strategy with an ethical agenda. A model of lightness, the metal dwelling openly avows its respect for its surroundings: since no tree was to be cut

down to make way for it, the trunks simply pass through the structure.

New concepts of habitat

The house is the exemplary individual venture and an inexhaustible terrain for experiment. The trend today is new loci for new lifestyles. Conceived specifically around the physical handicap of one of its users, Rem Koolhaas's celebrated Maison Lemoine at Floirac, near Bordeaux, offers innovation in the form of a mobile room, a space that moves up and down a wall of bookshelves. This feature apart, the overall concept can be summed up by the idea of the "flying box", with a long cantilever, designed by engineer Cecil Balmond.

Other houses have been designed with changing use in mind. Flexible space is the spirit of the villa Gary Chang built at the foot of the Great Wall of China (2003), which also plays with the cantilever notion. This "Suitcase House" opens and closes at both ground and roof level, testing out new living spaces. Thus its long open plan can be transformed into a sequence of areas in an architectural layering that can make all the various elements disappear, from the kitchen to the bedroom to the meditation nook. Then there remains only the wood that covers both inter-ior and exterior.

The Seifert & Stöckmann "Drawer House" at Gelnhausen in Germany (2004) seeks another kind of mobility in its expression of an irresistible urge to break out of the traditional house framework. The bedroom is a box on rollers that, with the help of an electric motor, can literally expand out into the exterior.

This kind of dynamic does not have to depend on mechanical aids: it can also take a purely spatial form, as in Odile Decq's scattered Rolling Stones project on a site at Nanjin, China (2003). With its contemporary "stones" that seem to be rolling down the slope, the system allows each person to live where he wants in an "à la carte" house designed for surprise and discovery. "Nomad housing", its French architect calls it.

Driven by lack of any real alternative, Monolab's facette house in Holland (2004) takes an opposite tack via ingenious means of grouping. On a tiny plot the architects have worked up a scenario that emphasises the living area by suspending it over a block containing more personal spaces. The terrace is equipped with a sliding tent.

Still in Holland, at Hilversum, Nio Architecten have taken up the challenge of building

106

107

ARCHITECTURE GOES GREEN
106+107. **Mixed-function building in Nantes, France, by Tertrarc.** At the base of the Tour de Bretagne, its slanting, coloured posts and fragmented-volume upper level give this corner building the look of a series of sedimentary layers. The triple strata effect offered to the passer-by comprises housing on top, shops at the bottom, and offices in between. The apartment gardens and terraces make this a country nook in the heart of the city.

108

109

OF SAND AND STRAW

108>111. **House in London, by Sarah Wigglesworth.** Built by the architect for her personal use, the house comes in two parts: the architecture studio and the residence proper. The little tower on top is a home for books. Set on a former brownfield site north of the city, this low-tech venture makes maximum use of cheap and recycled materials. There's also a little echo of the London Blitz: one facade is composed of stacked sandbags, while another is kitted out with bundles of straw.

110

111

112

next to a motorway with a dozen "Cyclop's houses" set out in a defensive herringbone pattern. Theoretically more utopian, François Seigneur's Autologement project of 1999, which allows you to park your car in your apartment, transcends the car cult in the context of a conscious move towards the future. Note, though, that the project is designed for "clean", i.e. electric vehicles.

In praise of the ordinary

The Anglo-American architect and critic Charles Jencks saw the death of modern architecture in the 1972 demolition of the Pruitt-Igoe high rise project – designed by Minoru Yamasaki, he of the Twin Towers – in Saint Louis in the United States. Since then, the rise of heritage consciousness has gained the modern era and the 20th century, now definitively seen as part of the past. The page has been turned and contemporary art photographers Bernd and Hilla Becher have spared no effort to inventory water towers, pitheads and other industrial monuments in building their record of a great era.

Sites revitalised, buildings regenerated: the examples are already beyond counting. London's Tate Modern, the transformation of an 1930s power station into a museum by Herzog & de Meuron, marks the rebirth of a 20th-century industrial cathedral. The spectacular changes wrought among Germany's Ruhr plants involve multiple forms of rehabilitation: one case in point is the 100 metre high gasometer at Oberhausen, artistically tweaked by Christo in the 90s with his giant interior wall of coloured fuel containers; another is the Zollverein site, once Germany's biggest mine, whose design museum segment was entrusted to Norman Foster in 1996. The redevelopment masterplan was the work of Rem Koolhaas, while Kazuyo Sejima is going to provide a 36 metre high white cube to house a new school of design.

Fruit of the rehabilitation of a biscuit factory on the banks of the Hudson, the new Dia Center in New York State (2003) is a recent addition to the long list of industrial conversions since the 1980s. Dia: Beacon is a museum, but an undesigned one, the young New York team Open Office and Californian artist Robert Irwin having settled simply for revealing the existing space. In Beijing, Chinese artists have likewise opted to set up in a factory, a kind of late-Bauhaus 50s building renovated for cultural purposes in the city's Dashanzi district, far from downtown.

The splendid transformation of Vicenza's Basilica by Palladio, and the grandiose mutation of the Theatre of Marcellus in Rome into a palace for living in are useful reminders that architecture has always been driven by the absolute necessity for evolution of the heritage – the need to make it live, and live on. What's new these days, though, is the trend towards recycling of unattractive buildings, following in the footsteps of Robert Venturi and his advocacy of working with "the ordinary and the ugly".

Relevant here is the return of the container. In this field, standardisation on a world scale began with the appearance of the first container transport in 1958. It's hard to imagine a more basic element. Despite the regular news reports of unfortunates dying in the course of attempted frontier crossings in containers, and the fact the American prison at Guantánamo was put together out of cut-up containers, they have also found their use as habitat. And while Didier Faustino created the event of the 2000 Venice Architecture Biennale with his Body in Transit and its container-related question about the human body in peril, in the mid-90s architects Marzelle & Manescau had already taken out the Europan Prize with a project for a container habitat in Rotterdam. They later went on to produce a modified version for Bordeaux's Chartrons district, a stone's throw from the river Garonne, in response to a brief for a Sonacotra workers' hostel. While American architect Wes Jones bends his imagination to creating a mobile, habitable, container-based environment, another specialist, Han Slawik used containers to bring real architectural dignity to resolving the plight of homeless children in Hanover (2002). The same year saw the advent of Cocobello, a mobile, telescopic "flexible unit": the work of German architect Peter Haimerl, this down-to-earth container-influenced project offers possibilities as housing, offices and other uses. And, in the artistic field, Shigeru Ban created a Nomadic Museum, composed only of containers...

A basic survival component, the container has become a true urban entity. Without any real recourse to architecture, the idea was concretised in London, east of Canary Wharf, where Container City is composed of fifty or so coloured boxes with big portholes cut into them. Not altogether unexpectedly, the same rationale applied to Rotterdam, Europe's largest container port, resulted in MVRDV's multicoloured Container City installation of

113

CONCEPT HOUSES
112+113.
The "Suitcase House" at the foot of the Great Wall of China, by Gary Chang. This is one of the nine dwellings making up the luxury "Commune" estate north of Beijing. Long (30 x 6 metres), cantilevered and resting on a concrete block, it has a railway wagon look that invites the beholder to get on board. Steel frame, all-teak covering and a single space given total flexibility by a system of movable panels and pneumatic jacks: the floor opens up, for example, revealing bookshelves, kitchen, bathroom, multimedia space and meditation room. All this with an escalator leading up to the panoramic terrace.

Following pages.
THE CHECKERBOARD STRATEGY
114+115. **The "Drawer House" at Gelnhaussen, Germany, by Seifert & Stöckmann.** In this historic village not far from Frankfurt, the architects used an earlier, demolished house as the imaginative launchpad for a project they called "Living Room". With no distinction between facade and roof, unity is achieved using a white aluminium skin punctuated by 52 identical windows. The building's most unique feature is a fully usable, 22 square metre mobile room: running on rails, it moves out like an electrically driven drawer five metres above the street.

116

AN ISLAND ON THE ROOF

116+117. **House at Saint-Cyr-Les-Lecques, France, by Julien Montfort.** No effort was spared in this spectacular transformation of the original 1970s house. (Re)designed to make the most of the local landscape, the new version strives to blur the boundaries between inside and outside. The two eyes of the bathroom look outwards and a metal portico means the glass wall of the top floor can slide vertically upwards. The roof is entirely taken up by the swimming pool, reached by a staircase leading to a teak island-platform. Here you can swim in utter privacy: only the horizon can see you.

117

118

FRAMING THE VIEW

118+119. **The home of a film director in Porto, Portugal, by Souto de Moura.** Totally zinc-clad, this highly cinematic house is characterised by its determined avoidance of banality. The challenge for the architect was to exclude the view of two neighbouring 15-storey tower blocks. The solution was a distinctive visual and spatial framing of the view of the city, obtained by dividing the library in two.

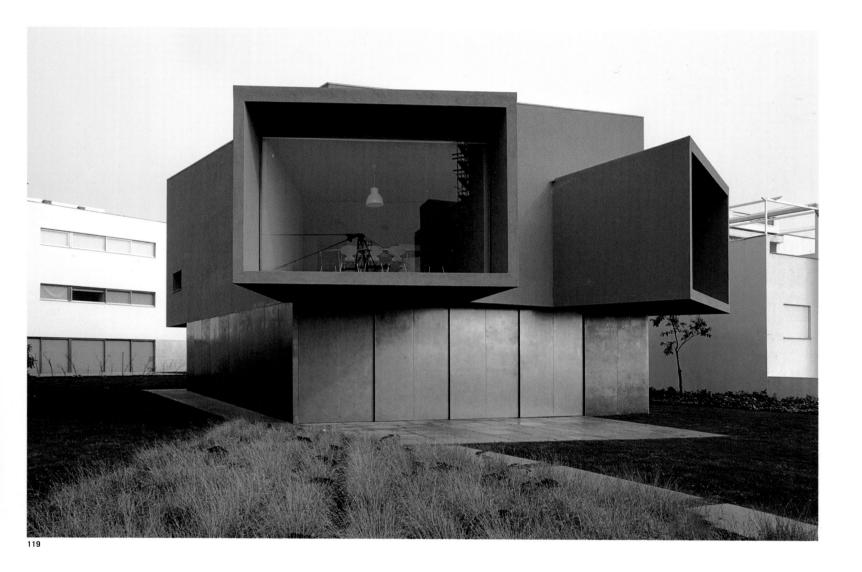

119

120

2002; sticking to the simple principle of stacking, Winy Maas's team played with 3,500 standardised units. In 2003 MVRDV got serious about the idea with its Silodam operation, a group of 157 apartments, plus offices and shops, stacked on piles. Each function was given its colour code.

Unlikely but not unfeasible

The name of the game, then, is improving the banal. The sign of the new trend came with the Le Fresnoy studio at Tourcoing in northern France, a centre for cultural experimentation (re)designed in 1997 by Bernard Tschumi. Here a side-by-side series of buildings making up a leisure complex of no particular interest has been given a breathtaking new lease of life in the context of an art school devised by Alain Fleischer. The new building, outcome of a competition with a clear demarcation between demolishers and converters, embodies a triple attitude: preservation of the site's history as a popular entertainment centre; the envelope strategy, with a second roof unifying the various buildings; and the "in between" idea so dear to Tschumi, with the opportunity to create an itinerary of walkways between the old tiled roofs and the vast high-tech canopy.

In 2001 Philippe Gazeau won France's Silver T-Square prize for his spectacular reworking of a frankly ugly 1940s sports building at one of Paris's northern gates. He retained only the essentials of the original, stripping it naked and transfiguring it by grafting on a new gallery wrapped in a translucent plastic skin. He then extended the idea to a new building, the Médiathèque at Mouans-Sartoux in the south of France (2002), which he treated in an industrial vein, with concrete and polycarbonate. He showed no misgivings about putting the downpipes from the guttering on display, giving them a soft look that gives a certain strangeness to what is a local cultural venue.

A similar kind of thinking is apparent in the French embassy in Warsaw (2004), but here the stakes were different: Jean-Philippe Pargade's slant on revitalising Bernard Zehrfuss' hyper-Cold War architecture involved a real challenge. The building might have been unattractive, but its Prouvé panel design was sound and Pargade set out to highlight the panels with micronised particles derived from aeronautics. A fringe of cut glass in the lower part of the metal carapace brings new eloquence to a building that for a long time had nothing to say for itself.

121

BRINGING GENIUS TO THE SMALL PLOT
121. **The "Body House" in Rotterdam, Holland, by Monolab.**
Small budget, big potential: how to fit 156 square metres on a plot measuring 6 x 13 metres. With the human body as its theme, the scenario provides a metal-frame house whose "heart"– notably in the kitchen and dining room – is optimal living. The faceted streetside "eye" has something of the insect world about it.

Facing page.
120. **The "Mini" house in Tokyo, Japan, by Bow-Wow.**
A made-to-measure metal house that gets the most out of the available space – with the cantilever creating a shelter for the eponymous Mini.

122

123

TOTAL PLASTIC
122. House in Tokyo, by Masaki Endo.
Ellipsoidal, experimental and anchored to the slope of the busy Shibuya neighbourhood. Here the quest for privacy is taken to radical lengths. Equipped with virtually a single, ultra-narrow window, the three-level house takes its light from a well dug into the heart of the ellipse. Stretched over a metal skeleton, the plastic skin is a space research spin-off product.

THE FINE ART OF RECHANNELLING
123. The "Perfect House " module, Paris, by Combarel & Marrec. This structure is the result of the rechannelling of an industrial component – a skylight – into a global-function system: roof, floor, walls. Set on the ground, the assemblage of self-supporting elements offers an envelope opening every which way; and closed, it caresses its occupant with a film of diffuse light.
Design-wise the structure functions as a furniture-space incorporating a combined bath-bed-sofa.

THE PLACE IN A STATE OF FLUX
125>128. The Yokohama ferry terminal, Japan, by Moussavi & Zaera-Polo (FOA).
A building set on the water, a design guided by the dynamics of movement and various activities: transport, retailing, culture, etc. No less than 450 metres long, the oblong landing stage is home to a harbour station that most notably offers this port city a high-quality public space. In many places the vigorous metal frame, visible on the inside, is covered with wood: an echo of the ships of old and a link between indoors and outdoors.

Preceding double-page spread.
124. Between sea and sky: the terminal's vast wooden deck. Here the movement of both traveller and stroller responds to the interplay of the ramps, undulations and folds of this giant origami. With no real facades, the building nonetheless develops its "fifth facade" in a highly expressionistic way: the roof, the architects stress, is "the consequence of what happens underneath."

In Paris, where the Grands Moulins district near the new Bibliothèque Nationale is set to become a university campus, one of the major features was what rehabilitating architect Rudy Ricciotti termed the "concrete Quasimodo". His project set out to take full advantage of the impressive structure of the disused flour mills – concrete walls 80 centimetres thick – otherwise doomed to disappear. "It was the beauty of all that ugliness that I loved," commented Ricciotti.

In France, then, as in other countries, old carcasses get recycled, but a new slant on heritage means that surgery, whether invasive or cosmetic, does not exclude a return to lost aspects of use and urbanity. That, in fact, is what it's all about. Patrick Bouchain's Lieu Unique ("Unique Place", 1999), created on the famous LU biscuits industrial site in Nantes, had two things going for it: it avoided the demolition of a factory that was an integral part of the urban heritage, and made use of the "already there". The task, then, was to move in unobtrusively, to do only the minimum needed to recharge a site already vibrant with memories. The Lieu Unique set a precedent by proving that the project – in this case a cultural machine remarkable for its transversal effectiveness – is more important than the budget. Bouchain would apply the same

agenda on a larger scale at the Condition Publique in Roubaix (2004).

This type of operation remains controversial in Paris. In 2002 Lacaton & Vassal's conversion of the Palais de Tokyo, a handsome building, for the 1937 Universal Exhibition into a contemporary creation venue unexpectedly resulted in a kind of brownfield in a quietly chic part of the French capital. Working with an extremely meagre budget, the architects set out to bring the building into line with the norms by, among other things, stripping the marble "palace" back to its delicate concrete. The rest has to do with a concept ideally borrowed from the busy Djemaa El-Fna square in Marrakesh. Here minimalism made way for the bare minimum.

It should be noted that in Nantes, as in Paris, normal aesthetic considerations went out the window, to be replaced by an aesthetics of cost reduction. In its extensive borrowing from early Arte Povera, this vision of things is far from finding universal acceptance among architects, mostly unwilling to abandon the aesthetic dimension. "Architecture lives and survives through its beauty," affirmed Swiss architect Jacques Herzog when receiving his Pritzker Prize in 2001. Wholehearted subscribers to this point of view are Spaniards Mansilla & Tunon, creators of the markedly

Cubist auditorium in Leon (2001), a building that plays as much with light outside as it does with sound inside: "Beauty is something that has been absent from the architectural lexicon for years, and we have to find it again."

The era of the multifunctional
To design is to look ahead to the uses most likely to arise in the future. In other words, to create places capable of anticipating life's needs and styles. In Turin Fiat's Lingotto complex, that engineering masterpiece of the 1920s, was a trailblazer: the cars that rolled off the assembly line were tested on a special track with crash barriers on the roof. The building was an architectural celebration of productivity and speed.

In his 2003 conversion of the mythical plant into offices, shops, a hotel, a university, an auditorium, etc, Renzo Piano added a volume suspended over that famous roof. A visual reference to a toolbox, this blue object in fact houses a veritable treasure: the collection of former Fiat boss Giovanni Agnelli. And so with the passing of time Lingotto, an icon of industrial architecture, has become the archetype of the mix of functions.

Eighty years after the building of Lingotto, the winning entry in the Yokohama ferry ter-

125

126

127

128

130

131

UNDER THE ASPHALT, THE ART
129>131. **Art gallery at Tokamashi, Japan, by François Roche, with Stéphanie Lavaux, Jean Navarro and Pascal Bertholio (R&Sie).** Created by the distortion of an enormous gobbet of asphalt, the carpark lot rises to a height of 3.16 metres over exhibition areas giving onto the green of the surrounding landscape. In a striking aesthetic contrast, the inner surfaces of an area delimited by leaning columns is entirely covered with a textile membrane.

minal competition announced a new generation of projects (2002). It was neither more modern nor more futuristic than its rivals, but it embodied something more than mere functional values. Unable to settle for being a simple transport facility, it became a place for everybody and a real bonus for the city.

The work of London's FOA team, this sea terminal of another kind typifies the complexity that has marked the move from one century to another. First of all it is a public space, then a venue that lends itself to a mix of cultural functions and fashion parades. The agora, born of the hybridization of brief and forms, represents a novel topographical exercise, one of whose leading qualities is that it

ignores the urban anarchy outside. For the rest there is the sheer pleasure of being able to stroll amid its contour lines and stretch out on lawns set between sea and sky.

New species of spaces

A few years earlier several major buildings in Europe, very different in both brief and style, had begun to react to the new requirement for variety. French writer Georges Perec showed a pioneering alertness in 1974 when he wrote, in *Species of Spaces*: "Spaces have multiplied, fragmented, diversified. They now come in all shapes and sizes, for all uses and for all functions."

In Germany's reunified capital, Dominique Perrault's 1999 building provided a conceptual yet rational response to a "2 in 1" prerequisite by incorporating two major sporting facilities (a cycle track and a swimming pool) into a single structural base. This no less than radical project plays as much on the notion of territory as on unity of place, with the same metal mesh skin for the roof and the facade. And it throws in a thousand apple trees for good measure.

A very different strategy was used at the Lac des Quatre Cantons in Switzerland, where Jean Nouvel provided a "3 in 1" for the Lucerne Cultural Centre (1999). A museum, an auditorium and a multipurpose hall: Swiss hospitality under a broad, extra-thin roof. There's also the water that enters the building via a system of canals, in a deft bending of the "hands-off" rule regarding the nation's lakes. At Euralille, Rem Koolhaas' giant unifying

PAWING THE GROUND
132. **The cultural centre at Matsudai, Japan, by MVRDV.**
Not much sign here of the square plan this building
abides by, the geometry being no more than a catalyst for
the relevant flows. A network of axes intersecting at roof-
level gives rise to these six metal "paws" and the
impression that the centre is ready to start walking.
In addition to the panoramic viewpoint on the roof,
the building offers a public space at ground level.

132

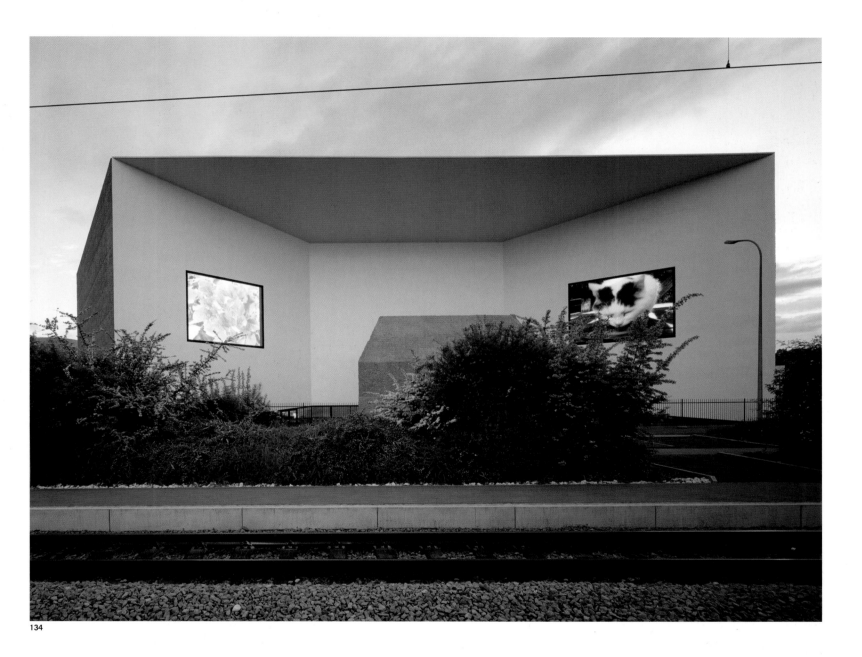

134

CLOSED: COME ON IN

133+134. The Emmanuel Hoffmann Foundation's "Schaulager" in Basel, Switzerland, by Herzog & de Meuron. A touch of the hybrid makes this a storehouse with a difference. Virtually windowless for a start, with just one long cut in its ochre concrete, it has a texture – the gravel from the excavation of the site – and a theatrical entrance that promise an atypical interior. What we have

here is a new concept: museum reserves you can visit. This means the works are not crated, but put on show in spaces whose mobile partitions offer real flexibility. Of the 12,000 square metres of exhibition space, over 7000 are devoted to the reserves. The floors of the three levels have been cut to provide an atrium involving the entire height of the building and it is here that the public is offered temporary exhibitions.

BEING ALONE IN COMPANY
135. A public space at Castelbranco, Portugal, by Didier Faustino (Bureau des Mésarchitectures). This architectural manifesto asserts itself as a "public space for individual use." Designed to accommodate a single basketball player, it has concrete stairs leading to a wire-mesh cage: usable sculpture in a social housing context.

ellipse (Lille Grand Palais, 1994) houses a Zénith concert hall, a convention centre and a trade fair hall. Apart from an extremely graphic roof, this event venue is wrapped in a translucent strip.

As for the Stade de France at St-Denis stadium on the edge of Paris (1998), the town planners had hoped that in addition to its sports occasions this would be a lived-in venue, with facades including offices and shops. Finally, however, they had to settle for a straightforward drawcard object, but with priority given to flexibility of use: soccer, athletics and festive events.

This mixing of functions is far from being a new idea, but the formalisation of the concept has changed radically. In Paris the Haussmann era had already explored the genre with its shops at street level and apartments above; and in Berlin the early 20th-century Hackesche Höfe ensemble was a marvellous mix of workshops, shops and housing in a succession of five interior courtyards.

However, the Yokohama terminal, a pure product of the computer, offered another kind of variety. It was no longer simply a question of broadening the cultural range as in Lucerne or Rome (the beetles of Renzo Piano's Parco della Musica, 2002), of providing sports facilities as in Berlin or an event venue as at Euralille, but of mixing and interbreeding

both the spaces and the people they would draw. This new kind of building sounded the death knell of the monocultural and monofunctional, and consigned Functionalism to its last resting place.

Thus venues are becoming more and more multifunctional and complementary. It's no longer rare to see golf being played on racetracks and bullrings temporarily turned over to concerts and tennis matches. The modern era is out to fill voids, and buildings' use-time is dealt with in a different spirit. So just as we've got chrono-urbanism, we've now got chrono-architecture.

Ineluctable hybridization

The "neither…nor" era is thus giving birth to briefs and buildings of steadily increasing complexity – and to another kind of architecture. As new lifestyles and urban living patterns develop, architecture is being acculturated, force-fed by all kinds of hybridizations.

One of the finest examples is Japan. A worthy heir to the Centre Pompidou in Paris, Toyo Ito's media centre in Sendai (2001) borrows the former's basic principles: structural intelligence, permeability between indoors and outdoors, and richness of intent. Add to this the fact that the Japanese architect called

in a different artist for each level – Kazuyo Sejima, Hanni Rachid, Ross Lovegrove and others – and you're looking at a project that is unique, inventive and thoroughly attuned to the contemporary city with which it sets out to establish a fulltime relationship. Its arborescent character – algae-like according to another interpretation – is the highlight of the whole thing, the aim being the new archetype announced by Toyo Ito: "A prototype for a structure that is as much a natural as an electronic flow."

The monolithic Schaulager art storage spaced in Basel (2003) might be at the other end of the scale in terms of form and intent, but it nonetheless represents a potently innovative concept – a kind of anti-Bilbao. Virtually without openings, except for an informal incision in its concrete, Herzog & de Meuron's block of matter has got what it takes to pull the passer-by up short. Once inside, however, you see what it's all about: museum reserves that can be visited, an idea pioneered by the artist Sarkis at the Centre Pompidou in the 1980s. In Basel the works are not crated, but visible and accessible in big spaces with movable partitions. This surprising museum gives the humble warehouse its letters of nobility.

It is true that art generates cyclical changes to its exhibition venues, but mobility is also a contributing factor in this kind of hybridiza-

136

WHEN FLUID MEETS RIGID

136. "Dock on the Seine": a project for a design and fashion centre, Paris, by Jakob & MacFarlane. Rather than demolish the early-20th-century warehouses, the architects came up with a 200-metre long scenario. The unattractive building turned out to be hiding a handsome carcass, whence the introduction of a fluid shape into a system of straight lines. The idea is to be up above the water; so a thick glass skin creates a volume and traffic itineraries. The aim with the roof is something more than a terrace: a veritable townsquare, in fact.

137

LIFE ABOARD A CONTAINER SHIP
137. **The Silodam in Amsterdam, by MVRDV.** A 10-level
urban "silo" on pilotis, designed for people wanting to live
and work on the water. All in all, 157 units from studio to
loft to business premises are to be found in this modular
ensemble that actually uses container colours. An
enormous teak deck is a reminder of the world of boats.

138

SPORTY COCKTAIL

138+139. The "Basket Bar" at the University of Utrecht, Holland, by NL Architects. Designed as a campus social centre and a meeting point for students, teachers and residents, this hybrid venue combines a basketball court and a bar, one on top of the other. The spreading roof of the bar offers a playing area 16 x 16 metres. Like the swimming pools you find in some bar-restaurants, the all-glass centre circle of the court establishes a relationship between two different activities.

139

140

SHARED TERRITORIES
140. **The Concept Office project, by Jacques Ferrier, France.**
Developed in concert with EDF, the French national electric company, this experimental venture offers 20,000 square metres of new-style workspaces. The glass-covering concept revolves around control of energy consumption and recourse to renewable energy sources – 80% of the heating, for example. In addition to this sustainability the concept focuses on space-sharing as a way of minimising space consumption. Set above ground level, the building is intended as an extension of the surrounding public space, which is open outside office hours.

Facing page
141. **Mixed-function building in Grenoble, France, by Héraut & Arnod.** What makes this corner building special is its variety of functions and typologies: a stacked-up mix of social and private housing, with retail outlets below.

tion. Shaped by Mies van der Rohe, the campus of the Illinois Institute of Technology in Chicago has seen Rem Koolhaas convert an abandoned site into something living: the vibrant McCormick Center (2003). Reversing his Euralille principle of the city plugged into the railway network, he has created an urban microcosm under a railway viaduct, with the plan determined by the lines of student movement. Incorporating an acoustic tube into its superstructure, the Center is a catalyst at the meeting of many paths.

Odile Decq and Benoit Cornette's viaduct at Nanterre on France's A14 motorway (1997) is the outcome of another form of hybridization, involving a bridge and an office block: the offices literally hang from the underside of the bridge, thus leaving room on the ground for development of public space around a historic road. The intention here is to leave the eye as free as the landscape and the approach reflects an ethics of avoiding uncontrolled land consumption. The "metropolitan gesture" of young Mexican architect Fernando Romero, founder of the Laboratory of the City of Mexico agency (LCM), is of quite another order.

His inhabited bridge on the Mexican-American border between El Paso and Juarez (2000) is a hybrid of bridge and museum, with the former suspending the latter along 180 metres over a large, multifunctional space.

On a more modest scale, MVRDV's cultural centre in Matsudai, Japan (2003) is an "octopus" with weird tentacles, traversed by three lines of movement: three bridges that seem to lift it into the air to create a protected public space.

These thoroughly site-specific buildings are a barometer of change. We can no longer assert, as did Sullivan in the early 20th century, that "form follows function", for all the indications now are that form follows movement – movement of the terrain in some cases, but mainly movement of people. How distant the time seems when train stations, new urban gateways set squarely in the heart of their cities, took on the aura of transport cathedrals, glorious celebrations of the industrial era. Those great urban halls are currently being replaced by buildings that are less typecast but richer in possibilities.

Ingenhoven's forthcoming station in Stuttgart might be buried 12 metres down, but it's far from blind, with enormous eyes looking up to the sky, which offer intriguing openings on a brand new public space. And while the station at Arnhem in Holland (UN Studio, 2005) mixes its functions in an interplay of curves defining a vast interior square, the stretched, hyperdynamic silhouette of the one in Naples (Zaha Hadid, project, 2003) is a response to the flow of high speed trains.

Cultivated oxymorons
Paradoxically, the stylistically rigorous Bibliothèque Nationale de France (1995), a Paris monument intended as the "founding act" for a new neighbourhood, is an attempt at hybridization. The insertion of a clump of forest reflects a mixed-genre agenda, even if, for the hyperrational Dominique Perrault, the result is not ambiguity but rather the idea of an aesthetic contrast between design and proliferation. Nonetheless, an impression remains of nature trapped inside built surroundings, of a project setting out to achieve a marriage of contraries. An eloquent forerunner of this kind of approach was Nam June Paik's 1977 *TV Garden*, with its extraordinary mix of the vegetal and the technological.

In contrast, Edouard François' housing project in Montpellier grabbed the headlines

141

142

143

in 2000 more for its updating of the private sector than for any real innovation within the apartments themselves. This was part of a new lifestyles strategy and the commercial success of a building dressed up in gabion panels and sold as "L'Immeuble qui pousse" (the apartment block that grows) is attributable to the in-between nature of the concept: the city with the advantages of the country, tree-houses, extensions to the living rooms that residents could reach via walkways.

Other experiments in Europe are overt examples of similar aspirations. Didier Faustino's Stairway to Heaven – a public space for personal use (Castello Branco, 2004) – has a sculptural staircase leading to an unusual sports area: a basketball basket in a cage...

Basketball also appears on the university campus in Utrecht, where the young Dutch team NL Architects has created a mixed facility – Basket Bar (2003) – in the form of a sports field sitting on a meeting place. The project was a response to the Rem Koolhaas OMA masterplan calling for "a rich mix or functions and urban programmes". The Basket Bar has been given the distinctive role of informal centre and catalyst for campus life: thus the café has an XXL, generously projecting roof which, transformed into a glass eye, establishes visual contact between bar and basketball court.

The phenomenon is also making headway in business property. In a field driven by optimal profitability, architecture has trouble finding its place: concepts have to fit with a basically contradictory dual goal – the corporate, with its call for specificity, and the speculative, which brings the banal in its wake – that has to anticipate unfavourable economic shifts. Given a situation in which factories are converted into museums and offices into apartments, why not plan ahead for this kind of hyperflexibility?

Jacques Ferrier's Concept Office, developed with EDF, the French electricity board, in 2004, fits this niche. With the notion of the domestic moving into the workplace, Ferrier proposes hybrid of office and urban space in experiments based on the theme of sharing. More research venture than architectural project, the idea, says its instigator, proceeds from the same principle as the concept car in its own field. Apart from its emphasis on energy saving, the project explores a new way of designing and organising work spaces so as to better share out the building, given that an office block is generally used at only 30% of

144

AT THE CROSSROADS
142>144. McCormick Tribune Campus Center, Illinois Institute of Technology (IIT), Chicago, by Rem Koolhaas (OMA). Being a long way from a subway station doesn't stop this building from being in touch with the metropolitan flow, in the form of the to and fro of student life. Shutting out the noise of the passing trains by incorporating an "acoustic tube" in its superstructure, the Center functions around one of the original buildings designed by Mies van der Rohe, whose silkscreened portrait watches benevolently from the wall. Restaurants, cafeterias and "Internet pits" make this a great place for meeting and exchanging.

145

REAR WINDOW

145+146. **Group of apartments and shops at Groningen, Holland, by S 333.** On the fringe of a city centre it overtly sets out to reclaim for itself, this project is the fruit of the conversion of a 1.5-hectare brownfield site. A mix of 13 separate but overlapping entities provides a new semi-public space typology in the interplay of its very open interior courtyards. The diversity of the outer walls – glass blocks and gables made of cedar or covered with greenery – is counterpointed by the variety of the height and treatment of the terraces: "fifth facades" covered with gravel or lawn.

147

capacity. This division of territory – the equivalent of time-sharing in leisure accommodation – pans out at 56% office space, 26% group activities and 18% traffic areas. Placement within the building is aimed at mutual use of collective spaces.

The fifth element

Hybridization's dynamic, prospective side has at least two consequences. Firstly roof-use as part of the brief, and secondly the development of a "multilayered" architecture. Thus the marked trend to hybridization has reactivated the fifth element – the "fifth facade" that looks towards the sky. The era of the simple rooftop terrace is past: the roof is now an active component, an inhabited space. And things are really happening up there: with its scenic, look-no-hands staircase to the roof terrace, Alberto Libera's Villa Malaparte on Capri offers one of the handsomest fifth facades there is; you only have to look down from the mountain behind it to realise just how right this decision was.

More modest in its impact but just as radical in its concept, Julien Montfort's house at Saint-Cyr-Les-Lecques in France (2004) is another successful mise en scène, with its roof entirely given over to the swimming pool. Here the conversion of a 1970s dwelling gave the young architect the chance to rewrite a scenario, one of whose high points is a staircase opening onto the roof like an island in mid-pool.

Jean Nouvel's unsuccessful 2004 proposal for redevelopment of the Les Halles site in Paris takes up the roof theme on a grand scale: a fifth facade given poetic status with an extensive garden (and pool) suspended over a large atrium.

And the multilayering? When the MVRDV team pulled together the stacking idea into a utopia at the Expo 2000 in Hanover, they led the public through a Dutch pavilion designed as a series of strata: rock at the base, vegetal knolls on the roof, and fields of flowers and a fragment of forest in between. And windmills into the bargain.

In Nantes, Tetrarc skilfully managed coexistence between three functions: retailing, offices and accommodation. Situated at the foot of the unattractive Tour de Bretagne, itself set over a car park, their corner building (2003) generates an interesting face-off in typology of stacked building. Confronted with the same situation in Grenoble, Héraut and

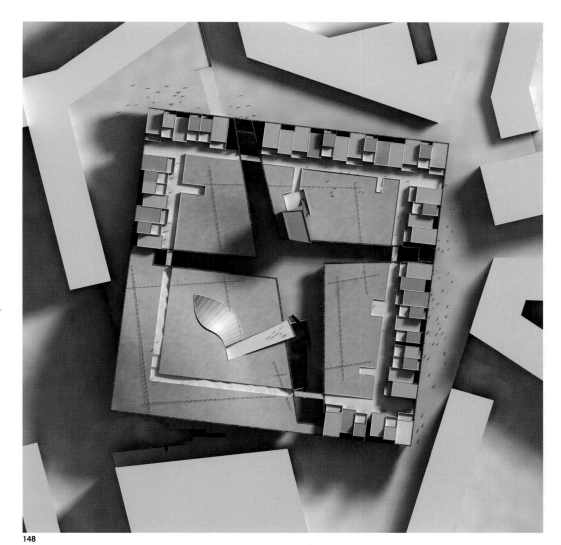

148

SWEET COMPLEXITY
147+148. Housing and shops in Almere, Holland, by Christian de Portzamparc. While returning to the spirit of one of his earliest successes – the La Roquette project in Paris – the French architect brings real variety to the old approach of traffic superposition and separation. Opting for a highly geometrical form – the square – he plays on alternation between levels and typologies. Set on its retail base, this grouping of residential volumes brings gently undulating roofing into the heart of the built area: a fifth facade with a country touch.

149

150

AMPHIBIOUS AMPHITHEATRES
150. **The Ponte Parodi project in Genoa, Italy,
by UN Studio.** Topographical architecture right here in the
port. As an interface between city and sea, the project
aims at playing its part in revitalising the Genoa shoreline.
With its vast platform devoted to retailing, technology and
leisure, the building also happens to be a terminal for
cruise liners. A whole raft of urban components for a
piazza by the sea.

Preceding double-page spread
149. The new face of Genoa's dockland. Gone are the
cathedral-like silos, replaced by horizontal structures
made with people in mind.

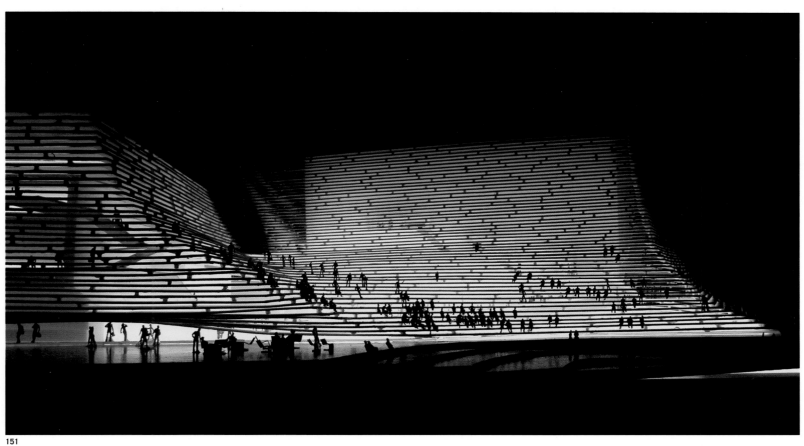

151

STEPPED FACADE

151. **Auditorium in Stavanger, Norway, by Plot.** Rejecting the idea of totally blocking the view of the fjord, this cultural facility highlights itself as a contribution to the spectacle. Playing an active part in the city, the concert hall is a kind of extension of a waterside urban park. Inspired by the terracing of ricefields, the architects have come up with a three-dimensional public space, an agora/building offering its stepped facade to the residents and the port itself.

152

YOU KNOW, YOU'VE GOT BEAUTIFUL EYES...
152+153. **The new station in Stuttgart, Germany, by Christoph Ingenhoven (Ingenhoven, Overdiek & Partners).**
Half covered market, half trench, the station has gone underground – 12 metres down – so the public space on its roof can merge with one of the city's parks while its enormous light wells also contribute to the effect at ground level. With Frei Otto handling the engineering, this is a "zero energy" station requiring no heating, no cooling and no ventilation measures: the prototype of the self-sufficient building.

153

154

RED CONNECTION
154>156. **The MACRO: the City of Rome Museum of Contemporary Art, by Odile Decq.** Overlap as a way of creating relationships in this extension and transformation of a 19th-century building: a basement 4 metres deep and a terrace – 3,600 square metres – available for public use outside museum hours. A real bonus for the city, especially with all the spaces being linked in a spiral. Not that much of this is visible from the outside: only a slim glass cornice and one transparent corner hint at the contemporary spirit of a museum making great play with the sensuality of its materials.

Arnod made the public car park part of the superstructure. Their "plate" serves as a terrace for a kind of strip-type social housing in a sculptural building that also includes privately owned apartments.

This kind of operation is only sporadic in France, but Holland seems to provide more fertile terrain, with the shortage of land conducive to compactness and complexity. In Groningen in 2003, the S333 team devised a very urban scenario in which public and private space discreetly intermingle: in all, a hundred units overlap with a shopping mall in a mix of the collective and the semi-individual. In the 1970s new town of Almere, now in a second phase orchestrated by Rem Koolhaas, Christian de Portzamparc is playing the stratification game by using the shopping mall as a base for the housing. In this harking-back to the slab base concept, the French architect nonetheless generates a whole new topography in the form of an undulating superstructure: the town with a view over the lake, and the countryside on the roof. The same concept has become even more intricate in Amsterdam, where NL Architects' Parkhouse project (1995) mixes architecture and infrastructure in an asphalt strip ensemble as complex in its form as in its content of offices, apartments and shops.

Moving right along

Layering is not only for functions, but also for networks. Thus we see the building treated like a ground-level prolongation of public space, except that this continuation often entails lifting. Topography is becoming more and more active, and we don't really need the Situationists to remind us that objects are less important than flows.

Like the Yokohama terminal, the Ponte Parodi, a vegetalised residential breakwater designed by UN Studio for the port of Genoa (2003) is based on the idea of topography for living in. The work of the Ben van Berkel team, it really stands out against the classical rehabilitation/reinterpretation approach applied to the Genoa docks by Renzo Piano.

A fresh kind of relationship is developing. Is it the proximity of water that induces today's architects to use the fifth facade as public space? Piano's science museum in Amsterdam, with its copper facades so openly suggesting a moored ship, does just this in the Venice of the North. Marseille's port terminal, designed by the young Lanoire & Courrian

155
156

157

A FEELING FOR TRAJECTORY

157+158. **The Dutch embassy in Berlin, by Rem Koolhaas and Ellen van Loon (OMA).** Redefining its own framework, the building feeds off multiple views of the reunified capital. As complex in its concept as it is compact in its form, the main cube offers the visitor a scenic itinerary, a "trajectory" that takes you up to a roof opening onto a terrace. The only cul de sac along the way is the spectacular metal and glass cantilever of the ambassador's conference room.

159

FROM RAMP TO BALCONY

159+160. **Junior high school in Santiago, Chile, by Mathias Klotz.** Out on the city limits and backing onto the mountains, this school makes the most of its elevated situation. The two classroom buildings are set traditionally around the schoolyard – but a schoolyard with real dynamism, creating its own slope with a raised slab over the gymnasium. And the ramp ends as a balcony, looking out over the countryside.

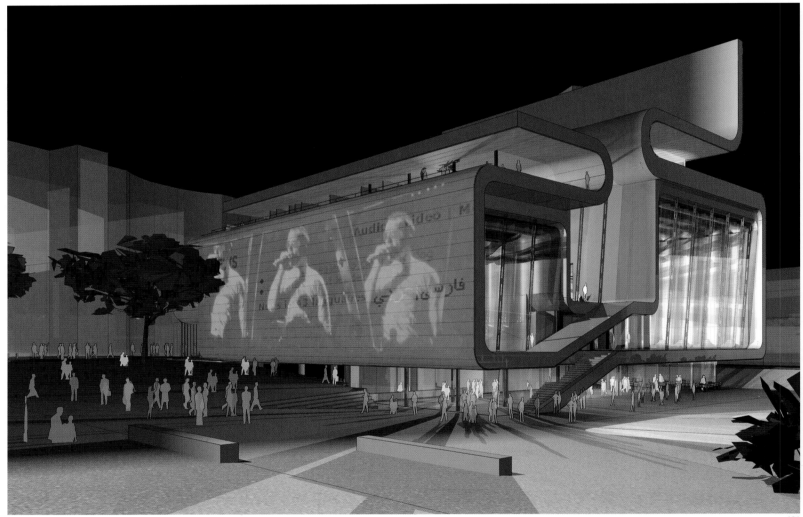

161

MEDIA BUILDING

161. **BBC White City, London, by FOA** Once off the ground, the building sets about playing with a continuous, conspicuously folded surface. The enveloping partitions of this "music box" work as floors, walls and roofs, with no break in the overall tempo. While the clear glass gables open the recording studios onto the city, the ribbon's opaque surfaces are used to achieve an effect of diffusion: thus the facades become vectors for images captured from indoors.

A PLEATED CURTAIN WALL

162+163. **The Citroen communication offices in Paris, by Manuelle Gautrand.** Right on the Champs-Elysées, this multifaceted strip makes as dynamic a showcase as you could wish for: 25 vertical metres of abstract play on the company's famous chevron logo, as a crystalline origami covers the facade, roof and rear of a building only 11 metres wide. And the cars? On show on an eight-level spiral display stand.

team in 2002, is less metaphorical, but still uses its roof as an interface between a city and its harbour. Two similar approaches have been tried in Scandinavia: in Oslo, Snohetta – he of the library at Alexandria – is using the roofs of the future opera house as mighty ramps plunging towards the fjord (project, 2000). Meanwhile at Stavanger in Norway, the Plot team's auditorium (project, 2003) plays a fundamental urban role with its stepped facades: the building itself disappears in this "total look" public space and the comments by its young Scandinavian designers leave no room for doubt: "The point is to consider the concert hall as an extension and augmentation of the movement and activity already produced by the site." This is also exactly what Diller & Scofidio are setting out do with their Lincoln Center in New York (opening 2008). In the heart of Manhattan's arts complex, a building with a gently folded roof offers access to two sloping lawn areas.

So architecture really is still hanging in there. Forty years after Brasilia and that magnificent slope leading to the parliament, Oscar Niemeyer surrounds his museum-flower at Niteroi, on the bay of Rio, with a spiral ramp. And much further south, in Santiago, Chile, Mathias Klotz has used the same idea for a different purpose: with its enormous ramp/courtyard, the Altamira College (2000) acts as interface, the slope changing into a balcony overlooking the city on one side and the mountains on the other.

There are also interior itineraries going back to the notion, so dear to Le Corbusier, of the "architectural promenade". The ramps at the Rotterdam Kunsthal (OMA, 1998) might only meet the requirement of connecting two street levels, but the Dutch embassy in Berlin (2003) has something very different to offer. The asphalt ramp from the street continues on into a specific network, as Rem Koolhaas & Ellen van Loon work on a trajectory concept whose complexity is due to a radical postulate: space dictates structure, and not the opposite. Here you see a Nazi building, there the East German TV tower, from a succession of points in which colour looms very large. One of these points is cantilevered, an hybrid excrescence on the cube of the embassy which projects an entire interior space out into the beyond. A conference room that also serves as dining room lets you go into town while staying where you are. The trajectory comes to a halt on the roof: a roof that opens to reveal an apartment for personnel.

162
163

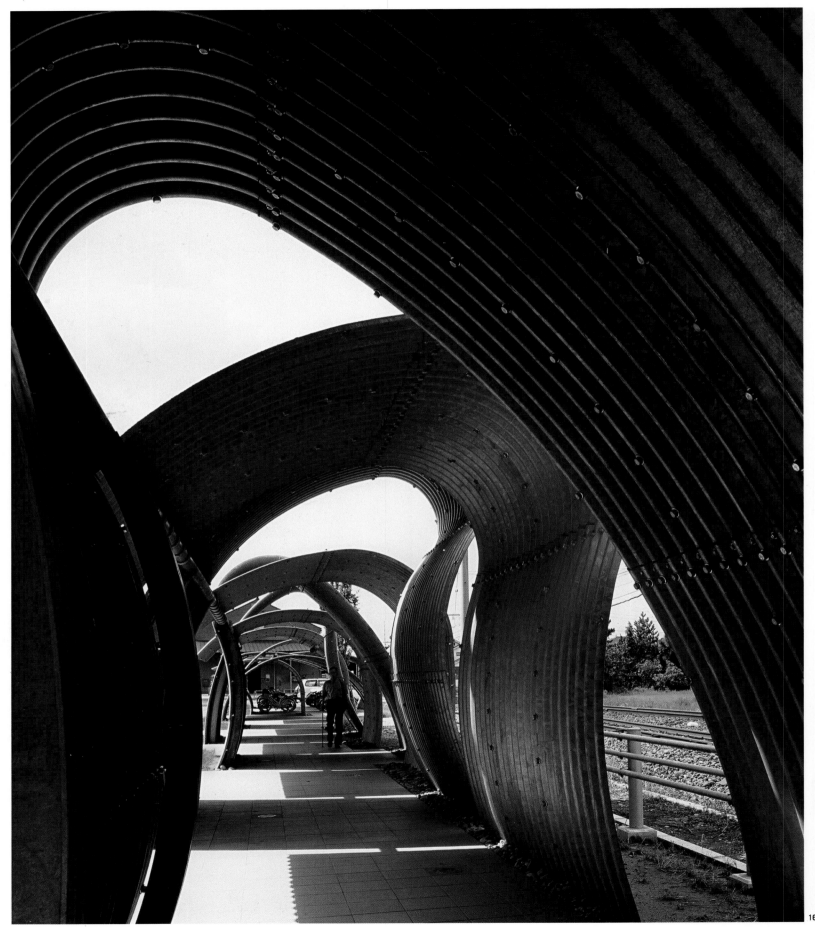

164

165

WAVES OF STEEL

164. **The station at Oozeki, Japan, by Shushei Endo.** This railway facility is an interface between the local houses and ricefields. Built exclusively of corrugated iron, the station – which also functions as a bicycle shelter – is aesthetically quite distinctive, with its curves and undulations providing the three basic forms of an architecture of lightness. Overtly inspired by the crests of waves, the movement it suggests is evocative of the mobile and the urbane: what might have been just a platform turns out to be a very convivial place indeed.

CORRUGATED RIBBON

165. **House at Biwa, Japan, by Shushei Endo.** The "continuous" space of this dwelling is the outcome of repeated bendings of a single strip of corrugated iron. The envelope moves smoothly over glass partitions and stone walls, leaving the occupant with an enormous feeling of freedom and comfort, the idea being to remove all distinction between inside and outside. The main architectural theme, however, is still that highly contemporary concern with eliminating the distinction between facade, floor and roof.

167

Odile Decq's 2002 proposal for an extension to the MACRO, the Rome's municipal museum of contemporary art, is based on an equally dynamic idea. Looking beyond the mere enlargement and modification of a 19th-century listed building, the project can only be understood as an itinerary: a museum itinerary informed by the sensuality of its material and the development of a rationale of ongoing movement and discovery along ramps ultimately leading to the roof. And there the visitor is presented with another contemporary universe: a terrace opening onto the Eternal City, a rare thing in Rome, where terraces tend to be for a happy few. Here the fifth facade, treated as a landscape in its own right, is surrounded by gables the architect sees as places to hang works of art.

Folds and Ripples

Even if eclecticism is the main sign of the times as the 21st century gets under way, still other possibilities are on the horizon for an architecture becoming steadily more complex. There are plenty of contemporary architects,

for example, who want a definitive end to the dictatorship of the box and the right angle. "Niemeyerisation" is under way, as today's practitioners mingle forms, interlock spaces and develop new in-betweens.

We seem at a far remove now from the Breuer who asserted that "Architecture must create forms that can stand repetition." In France the lycée at Nogent-le-Rotrou (BFT, 1995), with its sunbreaker facades and its pleasingly Donald Judd-like suspended boxes is a useful reminder of the aesthetic-rhythmic pairing. Even if the serial effect – the bar code as the dominant shaper of facade – is still as sure a bet as ever, the trend is clear: the trend to waves and folds, as if architecture wants to show itself perhaps not less brutalist, but at least more supple – even, soft – in its forms.

Looking back to the origins of softness and the fold, the list of buildings could include Philippe Starck's Nani Nani (Tokyo, 1989), a biomorphic echo of Japanese ghosts, or Peter Eisenman's prismatic but unbuilt Max Reinhardt Haus tower (1992) on the site of Poelzig's Schauspielhaus in Berlin. In both

NATURAL EXTENSION
167+168. **Project for the Launig Museum at Neuhaus, Austria, by Odile Decq (ODBC).** Melding with its surroundings, the white concrete building seems to rise out of the contours of the terrain, looking out across the valley as its folds and draperies gently turn into an exhibition space. The resultant envelope is a half-way structure that seems made for artistic strolling and meditation.

Preceding double-page spread.
THE SLAB LIVES ON
166. **The Paris transport authority centre at Thiais, France, by Combarel & Marrec.** With its "rising imprint", this building is determined to merge with its environment. The raised "parkabus" slab becomes the driver-reception area of a structure that rejects any idea of a beginning or an end. The building is a whole, right down to its bicycle/motorcycle shelter. Its thick grey coating formed from a near-liquid surface, it is encrusted with blocks of coloured glass, like radically cut precious stones.

169

BUSBLOB

169+170. Bus stop at Hoofddorp, Holland, by Nio Architecten. Urban-scale design using synthetics: in the middle of a big square a piece of foam-and-polystyrene urban furniture 50 metres long, a "blob generation" bus stop that in fact lends itself to all sorts of other uses: ask the local skateboarders, for example…

170

Italian Art, the answer is yes: "Forms dilate and multiply, their interlockings become entanglements… or they express a quivering or nervous vitality, a ceaseless, shifting need for generosity and movement. The concrete space of the building is taken over by imaginary spaces, both inside and outside." Two and a half centuries after the apogee of architecture and urbanism in Europe, we feel that same vitality, that same energy.

The envelope tendency

And what about the architecture/industrial design rapprochement? The current soft forms hark back to the Sacco beanbag seat of the 1970s (polystyrene balls that followed the line of the body) and the fold has found all sorts of uses in furniture. Gehry's folded cardboard chair with its seat made of three handsome loops can usefully be compared with Diller & Scofidio's Eyebeam art and technology museum project of 2001. Well before that was the three-curve Païmio chair designed by Alvar Aalto in 1931. And in between came Verner Panton's 1962 S chair, a tribute to Rietveld's celebrated Zig-Zag model; Ron Arad's Well Tempered Chair, in folded sheet steel; and the handsome alpha of Marc Newson's Wooden Chair (2000).

Inside today's buildings we now find countless fold and curve touches. The photographer's cyclorama is a great source of architectural inspiration as angles smooth out, merge into the surface with no breaks or joins and above all no recessed joints: an unrolled sheet, and that's all. The new spaces in the Pavillon de l'Arsenal in Paris (Finn Geipel and @@@, 2003) are directly derived from this photographic process, and the result is there in the fineness of the shell, a smooth Ductal skin taking off from floor and walls to bring unity to the ensemble.

Running counter to the yen for cantilevers, the envelope tendency is expanding. It's part of the trend launched by Koolhaas' Educatorium at the University of Utrecht (1997), in which the floor becomes wall then ceiling. After Neil Denari's experimental space at the Ma gallery in Tokyo (1996) and the Diller & Scofidio restaurant in the base of the Seagram building in New York (2000), even the (little) drawings room in the new architecture gallery at the V&A Museum in London (2004) has given in to the fashion for the smoothly curved fold. In the Q! Hotel in Berlin, the rooms designed by Graft (2004) are in quest

171

WHITE RIBBON ON THE BLACKTOP

171+172. **Bus stop at Casar de Caceres, Spain, by Justo Garcia Rubio.** An architect has a sculptural fling with a pair of loops made from the same white concrete ribbon. Apart from them, this continuous 34-metre-long surface for buses and waiting passengers has two glass walls and that's all. The bar and the toilets are underground: here you think as much of Niemeyer as of Saarinen.

cases great attention has been paid to the silhouette: intended (supposedly) to frighten in Japan, and to provide an enormous kaleidoscope in Germany.

A year after the Bilbao Guggenheim, the Kiasma museum opened in Helsinki, with American architect Steven Holl inviting the public to try a spatial experience that uses a twist effect to generate mystery and surprise. Twisted space is a theme that has been explored on various scales: the little footbridge linking two buildings at the Royal Ballet School in London (Wilkinson Eyre's Bridge of Aspiration, 2003); an architecture centre in Amsterdam (René van Zuuk's folded zinc sheet, 2004); a retail leisure facility near Alicante in Spain, a sort of twirled rocket 200 metres long by Toyo Ito (project 2003); or Santiago Calatrava's Twisted Torso, a 176 metre apartment tower at Malmö in Sweden (2005).

Does this signify a return to the baroque? If we follow art historian André Chastel in his

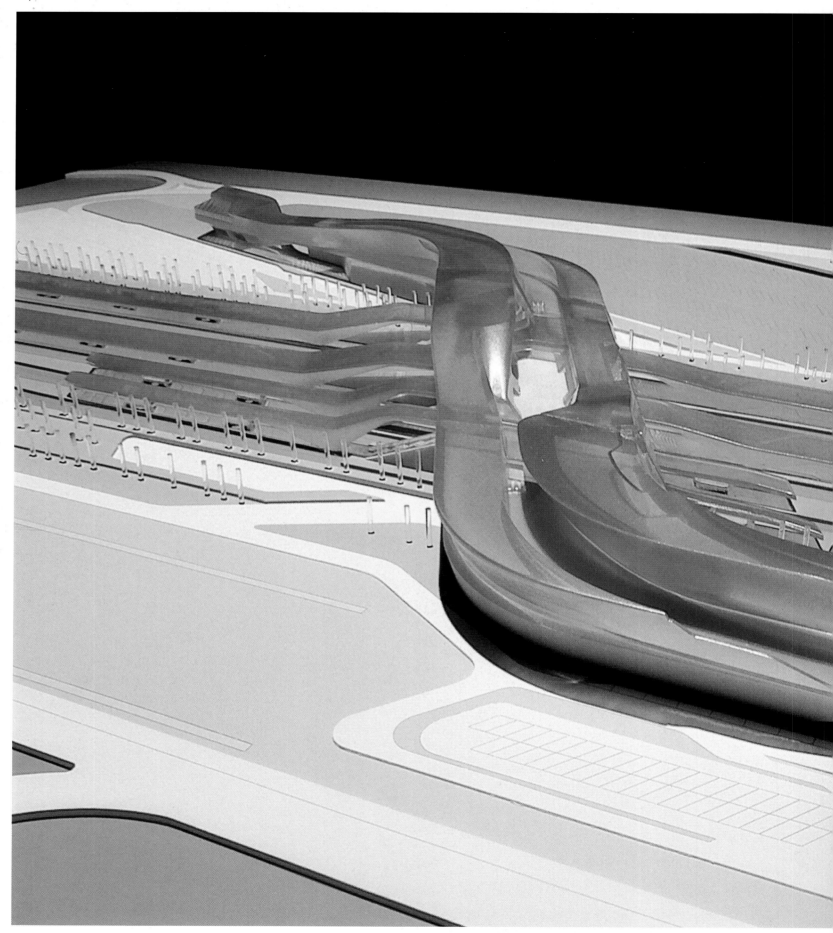

174

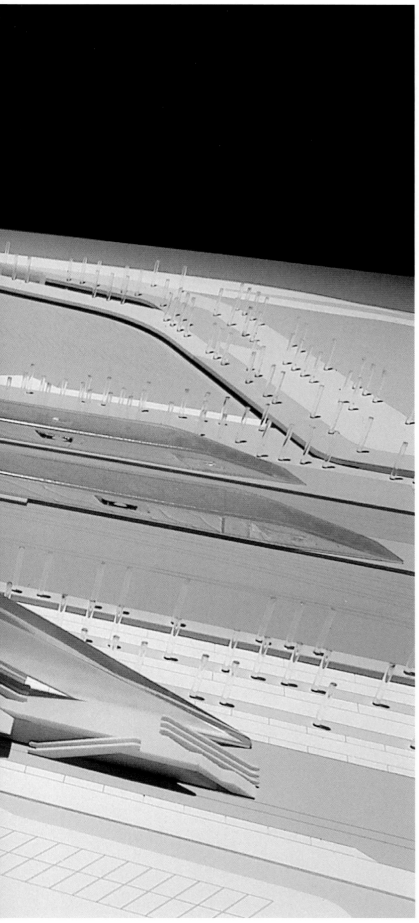

173

VIADUCT OVER THE TRACKS
173+174. **Project for a high-speed train station in Naples, Italy, by Zaha Hadid.** Planned to be operational in 2008, this new gateway to the city has been treated as a viaduct launched over the cluster of tracks. Non-linear and reptilian, the building is a link between two future urban hubs; and with its architecture wedded to the notion of speed, its interior design puts the passenger in movement straight away.

175

FULL LENGTH FEATURE
175. **The planned "envelope facade" for Ile Seguin at Boulogne-Billancourt, Paris, by Mathieu Poitevin, Stéphane Maupin and Jérôme Sans.** Following the curve of a bend in the Seine, the island was for decades the place where Renault cars were made. The idea here is to preserve the memory of the abandoned industrial fortress with a structure that literally "envelops" the envisaged property development programmes. Surrounded by walkways, the structure allows for a stroll above the water-level, where cafés and shops are seen as having their place.

of fusion between architecture and furniture. And so the bed merges into the bathtub...

Combining this spirit of continuity with an urge to dramatise space, Jakob & MacFarlane have come up with large, folded, sharp-angled panels for their extension to the saw-tooth roof of an industrial building, Claude Vasconi's iconic Metal 57 (1984), at Boulogne-Billancourt, near Paris.

Sometimes drawing on mathematics or philosophy, architects are working more and more on the notions of the crease and the strip. Manuelle Gautrand, for instance, unfolds a length of rippling glass along the Champs-Elysées (Citroën building, 2005) and FOA's forthcoming Music Box in London (project 2004) shows a marked fold in its facade. But in parallel with these plastic approaches, we note an enhanced relationship between architecture and the ground: the built object seems less "put there" and more in continuity with the ground. This is a way of erasing the frontier between the building and public space, between architecture and its landscape.

What's more, this seems to stimulate creativity rather than hamper it. We could begin with the aesthetic Rooftecture circumvolutions that give Shushei Endo such undisguised pleasure in his restoration of urbanity to a rural train station at Oozeki in Japan: a demonstration of how, with a single material – corrugated metal sheeting – you can create a true work of – yes – art. In roofing the experimental factory at Magdeburg, Germany, with coloured stripes, Sauerbruch & Hutton also play the continuity card, since there is no distinction made between facade and roof. Reminiscent of Bayadère fabrics, the covering rounds off the angles of this industrial building and gets rid of the traditional sharp-edge factory image.

In the way it seems to rise out of the ground, the RATP (Paris public transport) building at Thiais (Marrec & Combarel, project, 2004) affirms this reversal of the standard rationale. With the ground undulating upwards to form a bicycle park, the envelope of this grey building with inlaid cubes of coloured glass has rounded corners that avoid any break with the public space. "The idea," explain the architects, "is to belong more to the ground than to the aerial landscape." In Marseille, Zaha Hadid's tower, a key element of the Euroméditerranée port redevelopment, is also intended to give the feeling that the ground is rising to become architecture.

176

Along similar lines, in Utrecht, Holland, NL Architects' Cap Gemini campus sets five buildings in a rising and falling garden, generating waves in its own landscape.

In Austria, the Launig Collection, the museum of contemporary art in Neuhaus (project by Odile Decq, 2004), is intended as an anti-box: all we see are contour lines that metamorphose into volumes. With the topography dictating the architecture, the envelope in folds of white concrete is governed by the slope, triggering symbiosis with the setting.

THE SNAKE BITING ITS TAIL
176. **The Federal Environment Agency in Dessau, Germany, by Sauerbruch & Hutton.** The crucial issue here was sustainable development. Refusing to use the plot in its totality, the architects strove for maximum output per square metre while minimising the impact of a thoroughgoing conversion. Intended to house a personnel of 8,000, this coiled snake-building has 450 linear metres of frontage. Seen from the inside, the external wooden cladding offers an intriguing view across the atrium formed by a single building.

Preceding pages.
177+178. Alternately contracting and dilating, the space of this skylit street is animated by the interplay of the walkways that make this housing estate a place where you can communicate.

177

179

MESHING AND BRAIDING
179. **The winning project for the archeology museum at Lake Paladru, France, by Héraut & Arnod.** Nestled on the edge of the marsh, this long, long building is out for symbiosis with its aquatic setting. Its woven wood structure reminds the visitor of the basket-making techniques of old.

Facing page.
180. **Winning project for the Mucem – the Museum of European and Mediterranean Civilizations – in Marseille, by Rudi Ricciotti.** In a style reminiscent of Gothic lacework, the bearing capacity of the facade is tested here on a grand scale using reactive powder concrete. The enormous, high-tech mesh envelope has a bioclimatic function; and beneath it begins an zigzag itinerary – starting out over moats – to the roof.

This propensity to round off angles, to wrap, and to enhance spatial fluidity and continuity between ground and structure, generates a Möbius effect. And what works for a large auditorium is just as valid for a bus shelter. At Casar de Caseres in Spain, a bus station becomes sculpture. Visibly marked by Saarinen's famous airport terminal at JFK, New York, Gusto Garcia Rubio injects movement into a white concrete structure, the result being a double 34-metre loop: one surrounding the waiting area, the other surrounding the ensemble as it creates a path for the bus. This aesthetically striking piece of work (2004) leaves little room for the toilets, which, like the bar, are in the basement.

The bus station at Hoofddorp in Holland (Nio, 2004) is less flamboyantly lyrical, but betrays the same sculptural urge in its all-synthetic slipper shape: a 50-metre long polystyrene blob that forms a huge piece of urban furniture.

And even envelope facades

From fold to strip is the easiest of shifts. From ad hoc modulations to linear process, the concept is based on the same idea of formal suppleness, with no effort spared, it seems, to drive out discontinuity. In his own apartment in the old town in Barcelona, architect Enric Miralles has given a free hand to bookshelves that flow from one space to another, a totally novel strip of books; and a decade later in Hong Kong, Massimiliano Fuksas and Doriana Mandrelli laid out a "red ribbon" as a veritable guideline for the Armani boutique.

180

181

SPIDERWEB
181. **Angelin Prejlocaj's choreography centre at Aix-en-Provence, France, by Rudi Ricciotti.** Powerful – and paraseismic – this building sets out to dramatise its load-bearing system. The spiderweb structure of this 36 x 18 metre black block is multiple and broken up. "A real builder's building," says the architect, stressing that the concrete was poured on site, not prefabricated. Its facades may be holding it up, but the structure keeps a secret or two: the actual performance area is underground.

Facing page.
ANGLE FOLDS
182. **Seattle Library, by Rem Koolhaas (OMA).** In a context of tower blocks, this cultural facility stands out via its singularly complex shape. Wrapped in mesh, the building delights in its own overhangs and obliquenesses. The frame as such – engineered by Cecil Balmond – is the loadbearing skin, notably comprising crisscrossing metal beams. All the rest is pure transparence, in the interests of an optimal visual relationship with the city.

By contrast the architects of the Smarch team opted for a strip of matter. The station at Worb, near Bern in Switzerland, does everything it can to be much more than just a station: with its built-in train depot and car park, it is hyperfunctional in addition to being hyperaesthetic. It even plays music. All on its own, a slight dent in the facade, echoing the curve of the tracks, suffices to give this 130-metre building its specific dynamic. The facades, like the interior skins, are made of the same material: stainless steel strapwork.

In France the "envelope facade" of Ile Seguin at Boulogne-Billancourt marks the birth of a new concept. The organisers of the competition were obviously inspired by the success of the Scandinavian Embassy complex in Berlin (Berger et Parkinnen 1999), with its unifying copper strip. With the Tiergarten park opposite, the idea in the German capital had been to give expression to a single entity –

Scandinavian culture – while respecting the identity of each element. The outcome was six buildings set behind a skin that created a free, highly dynamic form.

Diversity in unity was also the theme for the Postdamer Platz neighbourhood in Berlin. Completed in 1990 to a global plan by Renzo Piano, the project was governed by a simple, but subtly shared-out principle: Piano imposed a vocabulary – terracotta – while leaving each participant (Rogers, Moneo, Isozaki et al) to create his own architecture over 600 metres. The overall result is a terracotta strip.

Back at Ile Seguin, the winning project by Poitevin Reynaud & Maupin (with artistic director Jérôme Sans) brought more substance to the subject. 30 metres deep, the envelope facade transcends the simple skin notion to become a thoroughgoing public space with dynamic ramps integrating leisure activity and retail elements. In this inhabited strip scenario the buildings to come will "clip onto" this eyecatching surround.

Embodying a more autonomous concept, the Federal Environment Agency building at Dessau in Germany (2004) – 450 metres of lively, coloured facade – looks like nothing so much as a snake biting its tail. Faced with the challenge of having to accommodate 800 personnel in a maximum of four stories, Sauerbruch and Hutton went for length, optimising efficiency while reducing impact.

Between mesh and mantilla
Never has there been so much talk about materiality: by which is meant more matter than material. Skin might be important today, but it has to be considered in terms of different thicknesses. The dermis beneath the epidermis. The mesh notion took shape in an architecture out to establish several networks, several layers of interpretation, and even several levels of comfort. Mesh, mantilla and other interweavings are all grist to the light-filtering mill.

Where mesh is concerned, the Moscow radio tower (Shukhov, 1922) springs to mind at once. The structure alone is enough to create this light building which is still a yardstick today. Eight decades later geometrical, load-bearing nets are featuring in flagship architectural objects: the Swiss Re tower in London (Foster, 2004), the diamonds of the Prada building in Tokyo (Herzog & de Meuron, 2003), and the Rem Koolhaas library in Seattle (2004), all folds and cantilevers.

183

BEHIND METAL TRACERY

183+184. The offices of the Ministry of Culture and Communication, Paris, by Francis Soler, with Frédéric Druot. A stone's throw from the minister's offices in the Palais Royal, the Bons Enfants block was a real poser in terms of detailed restructuring. Given its disparities – buildings of different heights and from different periods – the architect opted for an "overall restyling" of the existing heritage, covering it with an innovative stainless-steel mesh filter that, in addition to providing a global look, was meant to totally change people's perception of the building according to the light. The laser-cut patterns take their inspiration from the Palazzo del Te in Mantua, Italy. Behind the protective grid, ministry personnel work in a light-filled atmosphere created by a mix of transparent and translucent glass partitions. At the very heart of the block is springing up a southern forest of 170 square metres: an experimental garden born of a collaboration between landscaper Michel Desvigne and botanist Patrick Blanc.

Both rigid and permeable, the concrete coat of the future Museum of European and Mediterranean Civilisations in Marseille (project 2004) is being eagerly awaited, with its orientally inflected surface not unlike Gothic lacework. Rudy Ricciotti has announced it as "a building of stone and dust", well anchored in Marseille history. This block of matter 72 metres square by 24 metres high is precisely aligned with the historic fort onto which it is going to be grafted. A bioclimatic mantilla of extra-thin Ductal will counter the effects of wind and sun, and the mesh is thrown over a box containing the museum like a fisherman's net, with the link spanning a seawater moat.

Less elaborate but far more powerful-looking, the structural mesh of Ricciotti's Angelin Preljocaj dance centre in Aix-en-Provence transforms our impression of what might have been no more than a block. With its spidery black concrete frame, and the slope that continues the adjoining square, this is the high point of Oriol Bohigas' town plan for this new district of the city.

Like Scandinavian artist Olafur Eliasson and his woven environment, Herzog & de Meuron are working on the theme with all the strength of large scale steel mesh for the Olympic stadium in Beijing (opening 2008).

In the French Alps, on a site for which environmental compliance is a fundamental factor, the idea of weaving really comes into its own. Designed by Hérault and Arnod (project 2001), the museum in the Paladru archeological park sets out to achieve oneness with its aquatic surroundings. Like a reptile ready to spring into the marshes, their multipedal building flaunts a woven skin suggestive of primitive life-forms. For obvious ecological reasons, all the wood is untreated.

Weaving also appears in Metz, France, where the Centre Pompidou regional annex (Shigeru Ban and Jean de Gastines, project, 2003) looks like a hybrid form topped by a large wooden hat.

Mesh can also serve as a unifying factor, as Francis Soler has shown in Paris with the Bons Enfants block, home to the Ministry of Culture

184

a stone's throw from the Palais Royal. This is more than just a restructuring of a residential ensemble, for there is a real agenda involved, with the architect out to establish "a new relationship between heritage and modernity." Stainless steel mesh extended over 6,000 square metres of facades serves to unify five dissimilar buildings; and a 492-panel kinetic facade – it moves as the observer does – is intended as an alternative to the "facadism" currently flourishing in European capitals.

The decorative patterns cut into the metal are based on figures from Renaissance painting. At the foot of the Bibliothèque Nationale in Paris Francis Soler has already borrowed figures from the Palazzo del Te in Mantua,

Italy to enliven the facades of his apartment building. A century after Adolf Loos, responsible for the petty aphorism "Ornament is crime", the trend thus seems to be in the other direction. We should also take a look at the use of silkscreening by Herzog & de Meuron (Eberswalde library, Kottbuss city hall), by Manuelle Gautrand (the tollbooth barriers on France's A16 motorway), and by Wiel Arets (the UBU library in Utrecht, Holland). For the facades of their museum in Leon, Spain, Mansilla & Tunon sampled a fragment of the cathedral there, digitised it and then unfolded the result on large-scale panels of coloured glass. "We plundered history," says Luis Mansilla, openly acknowledging the borrowing.

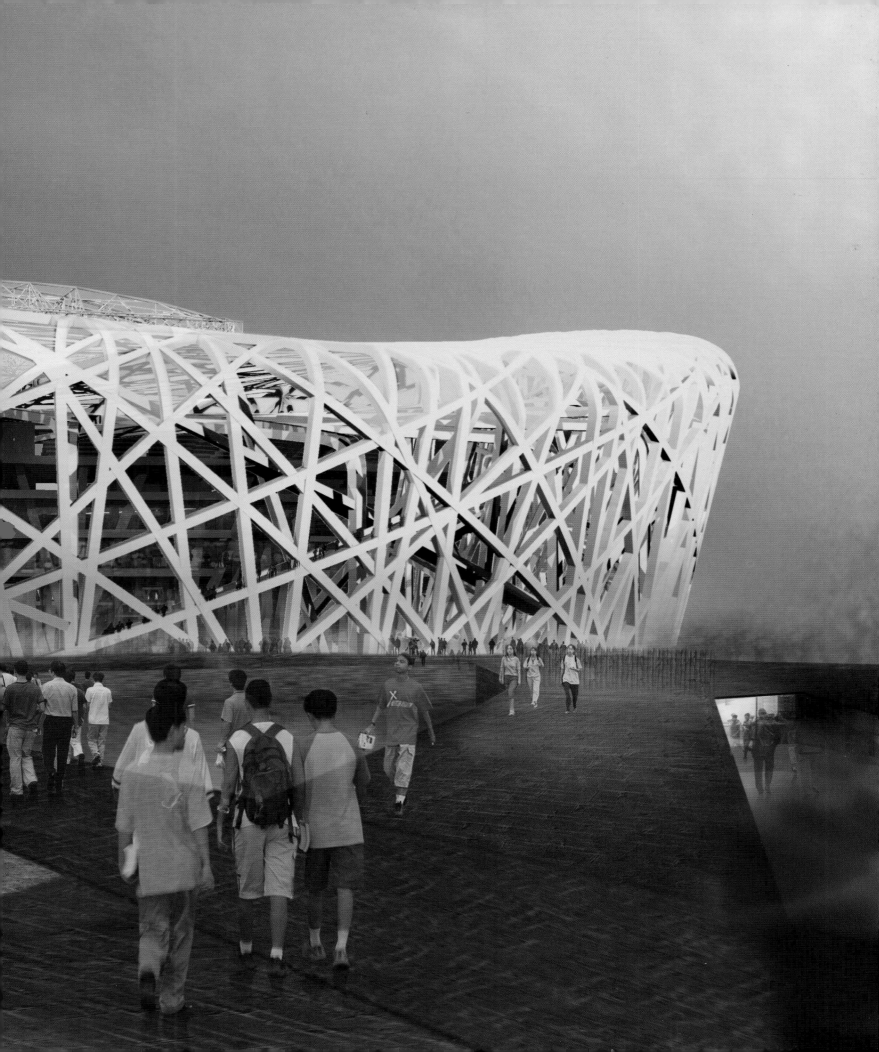

186

DRAGONFLY'S WING

186+187. The winning project for the new cinema centre on the Lido in Venice, by Rudi Ricciotti. Continuing his research into frameworks – alveolar in this case, to avoid the tensions of the usual steel stringers – the architect has found inspiration in the world of the organic.

BIRD'S NEST

185. The Stadium for the 2008 Beijing Olympics, by Herzog & de Meuron. This 100,000-seat arena is made up of a double envelope: a unifying mesh giving shape to this immense contemporary structure, and a simpler envelope. The nest's frame is a crisscrossing of leaning metal posts 1.2 metres square. It goes without saying that the complex frame-roof interplay betrays the hand of engineer Cecil Balmond.

187

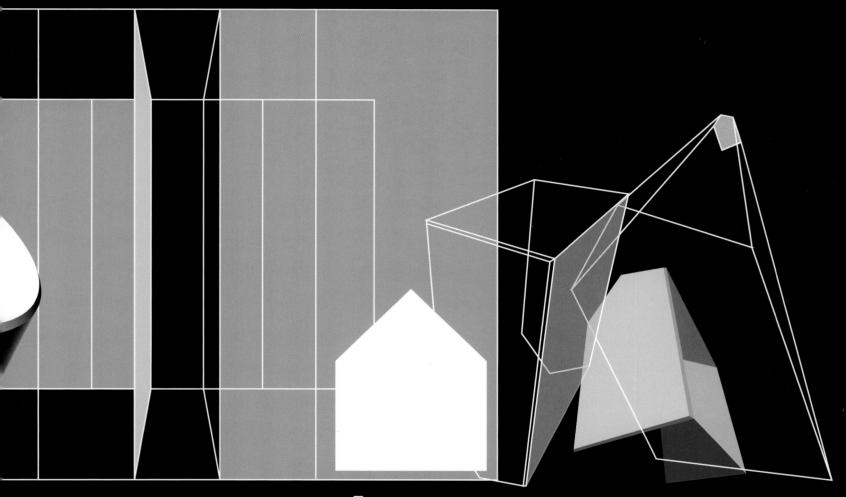

town planning: what now?

With sustainable development now a priority, the contemporary city is coming to grips with the great debate on density and urban sprawl. New tower concepts – less monolithic, more ecological – signal the post 9/11 era. And they are accompanied by a new generation of public spaces in which architects, landscapers and artists are playing a crucial role. With modernity now synonymous with mobility, urbanism equals nomadism. Architecture is going with the flow of the times.

chapter four

THE MILAN TRIO
188. "Citylife", urban project in Milan by Zaha Hadid,
Arata Isozaki, Daniel Libeskind and Pier Paolo Maggiora.
The land freed by Massimiliano Fuksas's Fiera di Milano
megaproject is witnessing the appearance of a new
planning approach, with mixed briefs countering with the
urge to leave a mark on the site. Whence this formal
exercise of three towers by three renowned architects.
To each his/her own mode of expression. Torsion for
Zaha Hadid (in the spirit of the future Marseille tower);
a curve for Daniel Libeskind; and something straighter
for Arata Isozaki.

With the backing of Tony Blair, Richard Rogers and the Urban Studies Task Force put a mighty effort into confronting today's planning issues and came up with the *Towards an Urban Renaissance* government white paper. In Holland Rem Koolhaas chose the city of Almere to implement a process derived from the circles of quality notion. And on the Tolbiac site in Paris, Christian de Portzamparc is setting about applying his "open block" theory in the field. Spirit and process, then, as urban form tries to make its way.

"I feel the certainty, or the hope, that the city of tomorrow will resemble that of the past, with its 'secret spaces'," said Renzo Piano, planner of the Potsdamer Platz in Berlin, in an interview in *Le Monde* in 1994. Ten years down the track we are facing the diffuse city and a change of scale: people act and think not in terms of a municipality, but of a micro-region. Farmland is being consumed by urbanisation, and urban sprawl, a factor in pollution and social inequality, is the new century's number one issue. Suburbia and "sprinkler cities" sum up urban sprawl as destruction of the agricultural landscape – and even of landscape, full stop.

No-Stop City (Archizoom 1969), Datatown (MVRDV 1999): For over thirty years the focus has remained the same, except that what seemed a vision then is tending to become reality today. With inner-city desertification a thing of the past and reclamation of our city centres well under way, the major concern for an era grappling with the issue of mobility is the outskirts. Taking a positive stance, Rem Koolhaas calls for a "*mise en scène* of uncertainty" and "channelling of potential into territories". China, a territory in a state of total evolution, seems especially open to this approach.

Did someone say sustainable? As the modern world's new paradigm, sustainable development extends beyond ecology to embrace the entire economy-society-environment trinity. When "bioclimatic" architecture came along in the early 80s, it represented an urgent response to the various oil crises, advocated alternative energy sources and found followers notably in Germany: Thomas Herzog and Rudolf Doernach, for instance. But the notion remained marginal and it was only in 1992 that the realisation really struck: that was the year when the whole world rushed to Spain to check out the ephemeral architecture of the Universal Exhibition in Seville and the permanent version thrown up by the Barcelona Olympiad; and when 170 heads of state met in Rio for the Earth Summit.

The greenhouse effect was growing, the balance of the planet was at risk, and the result was the concept of sustainable development. Here, development meant decompartmentalisation and progress could not be allowed to threaten the environmental balance in any way. Since then Richard Rogers has made the cause his own and Germany has become a fine example of prospecting for alternative lifestyles. On the fringes of Düsseldorf, the conversion of a former strategic nuclear site generated an approach all its own in 2004: for the move from missiles to housing the architecture competition – Tadao Ando, Thomas Herzog, Daniel Libeskind, Frei Otto and other participants – launched the 1 for 9 principle: one hectare

189

PIAZZA IN THE AIR

189+190. **Project for the London Bridge Tower, by Renzo Piano.** Understandably nicknamed "the shard of glass", this 306-metre skyscraper on the banks of the Thames is going to be Europe's tallest. A vertical city for a population of 7,000, it will cater to a wide variety of functions: offices, shops, apartments, hotels, restaurants, an auditorium, a museum, and more. One of its features is a public space halfway up.

built for nine given back to nature. In China the "ecological corridor" has emerged, as in Shanghai's plan for the conversion of a 600 hectare military base north of the megalopolis. In France the *coulée verte* ("green belt") idea is generating intermunicipal projects. There are no frontiers for urban ecology, which is now a long way from the romantic old idea of greening architecture and the city. But it still remains to be seen if ecologically correct is synonymous with architecturally correct.

The "sustainable city" concept is beginning to take shape. Friburg in Germany is one of the pioneers in ecological architecture, and Bed Zed is the benchmark operation in the UK, where Zed = Zero Energy Development. Sutton, in the southern suburbs of London has a typologically diverse ecological estate created by the team of architect Bill Dunster (2001), with 82 apartments and houses. In Finland the Vikki operation on the outskirts of Helsinki involves development of a sustainable site of 1,000 hectares. Sustainability and urbanity are now seen as going hand in hand: "Urbanism might be dead," says Patrick Berger, designer of the UEFA headquarters in Nyon, Switzerland (2002), "but urbanity is not. Urbanity means respecting urban principles so that we can survive in the future."

The rise of the museum city

Venice in Las Vegas, Colmar in Malaysia: heritage hijacked by tourism, stripped of meaning and disembodied in the name of image. And this in parallel with the museification of our cities. What major capital is still without its double-decker bus tour?

Heading down the nostalgia trail, we can visit the neo-18th-century village of Poundbury, near Dorchester in England, commissioned from Leon Krier by Prince Charles. The same agenda is at work in Brussels' Laekenstraat. But there is a distinction to be made between the "museum city" and such open-air museums as Miami's South Beach Art Deco neighbourhood, Casablanca, Chandigarh, Brasilia, the Tel Aviv of the 20s-40s, and Le Havre remodelled after World War II by Auguste Perret.

The dawn of the 21st century finds historian François Loyer observing that "We have to get back to the humble fact that successful architecture, contrary perhaps to the other arts, is always a product of social consensus." Does creativity still have its place in such a context? This is no trivial question, with architecture increasingly faced with the Nimby mentality of residents' associations out to halt ingress by any foreign body. Subjectivity rules. Whether the issue is that of Daniel Libeskind's controversial extension to

190

the Victoria and Albert Museum in London, or the (discreet) housing ensemble built by Herzog & de Meuron in Paris' 14th arrondissement in the early 2000s, the problem is the same, and town planning battles are far from over.

The current "juridicalisation" of architecture is not a good sign. Like publishers who call in lawyers for pre-publication readings of controversial books, architects are now having specialists check their projects out in the tiniest legal detail. The trend is more and more towards a cumbrous process of negotiation.

Our new century is hardly one of grand gestures or radical undertakings. This is an era of consensus urbanism, even if China is witnessing the first stirrings of what its leaders call "conceptual urbanism" as a replacement for the idea of planning. In Europe urban concepts are out: a consequence of the collapse of ideology and the end of all utopias?

In France, districts such as Le Mirail in Toulouse (1970s), Ricardo Bofill's Antigone in Montpellier, and Rem Koolhaas' Euralille, an experimental hypercongestion scenario designed to produce a "tertiary sector turbine" in the 90s, mark the end of this kind of ambitious – and a tad megalomaniacal – urban planning. Euralille was a first in France in involving a circle of quality. A concept neighbourhood if ever there was one, it will remain an example of a scenography of networks and infrastructures. "In the contemporary world," Rem Koolhaas explained regarding Euralille in 1988, "projects become abstract in the sense that they are no longer tied to a specific place or city. Instead, they float opportunistically around the place offering the most connections." Begun with the new century, Euralille's second phase is part of a link-based agenda with, notably, the creation of a new type of garden city – an inhabited forest – just beyond the ellipse of the Koolhaas convention centre: continuity rather than cut.

At the same time, east of Beijing, the high-rise estate from developer Soho (700,000 square metres, 2004) opens fresh horizons. Combining diversity of height, pronounced unity of facade and purity of presentation, Rikken Yamamoto's small-tower landscape – 100 metres maximum – offers a sound urban dynamic. The units rise

192

PORT PLATFORMS
191+192. **The winning project for the sea and sustainable development center in Le Havre, France, by Jean Nouvel.**
Facing the city rebuilt by Auguste Perret in pink concrete, a 120-metre tower is getting ready to leave its stamp on the southern skyline. Drawing on the aesthetics of offshore drilling rigs, this megastructure in the 19th-century dockland area is in fact a dual platform: 1,200 square metres at a height of 55 metres, and 2,000 square metres at 90 metres up. Totally glazed facades give a 360° view that includes the port and the Seine estuary. At the foot of this enormous contemporary look-out, the aquatic complex proper is taking shape – including, on the other side of the dock, a building whose randomly pierced concrete walls are said by their designer to be "inspired by Roman baths."

FRATERNAL TWINS

193+194. Winning project for the Central European Bank in Frankfurt, Germany, by Coop Himmelb(l)au. Something new on the skyline in Germany's financial capital: a building based on the notion of twinning. The two non-identical twins are united by a central atrium, an enormous transparent emptiness traversed by walkways. The vertical section fits perfectly with a horizontal structure housing the conference centre.

through a layer of walkways and planted patios, and remain in close contact with the retail outlets forming their base, the work of another Franco-Japanese team, Manuel Tardits/Mikan.

It will be interesting to follow the development of the "macroblock" concept as it is tested out in Lyon's new urban district "Confluence" with a bunch of architects after a general matrix by MVRDV The idea is to produce variety in a very rational project.

Memory matters

We're now looking at a different relationship with history. Christo might wrap the Reichstag in Berlin, but the duty to memory is tending to counterbalance the weight of history in the architecture field. French poet Paul Valéry once said, "Memory is the future of the past."

Let's return to Ile Seguin, a 1.2 kilometre long island on the Seine at Boulogne-Billancourt. When the massive Renault car factory was demolished after prolonged controversy, the site Jean Nouvel called "the collapse of the workers' world" seemed to have revived the debate begun 30 years earlier with the massacre of the Baltard pavilions at Les Halles. However the Ile Seguin's buildings could not be compared to those 19th-century iron umbrellas, or even to Fiat's Lingotto building in Turin. The idea finally adopted for the site was that of preserving the memory of its form. This notion of an architectural ghost was the source of the "envelope facade" intended to ring the island, otherwise to be occupied by Tadao Ando's monumental and recently

abandoned Pinault Foundation. Among the countless proposals for conversion of the island, the one by Renzo Piano suggested retaining not the original building but its shape.

Changing the content while preserving the memory of the form was Tania Congko and Pierre Gautier's winning strategy in the Europan competition for the Zaanstad site in Holland in 2000, where they retained only the silhouette of the factories in creating a set of 100 waterside housing units. Thus housing has taken over from industry: demolished or redeveloped, the workshops have changed their function, apart from the fact that their image remains familiar to the people who now live in them.

The debate over the rebuilding of the World Trade Center site was much more hectic and really mobilised an architectural community, at the urging firstly of the Protech Gallery in New York, and then of officialdom. Proposals poured in, freestyle, generous, and crazy: among them were Jakob & MacFarlane's giant algae and Nox's enormous root tracery. Ultimately the official competition was won by Daniel Libeskind in 2003: a crescendo of towers around a public space, a memory site with a "wedge of light" calculated according to the angle of sunlight on 11 September. But nothing could have been more beautiful than Julian La Verdière's "Towers of Light", two luminous columns rising into the immensity of the New York sky: a giant installation and a hymn to virtuality. This was the memory of form taken to the point of paroxysm.

Then came the 5,201 projects for the memorial (the Centre Pompidou had attract-

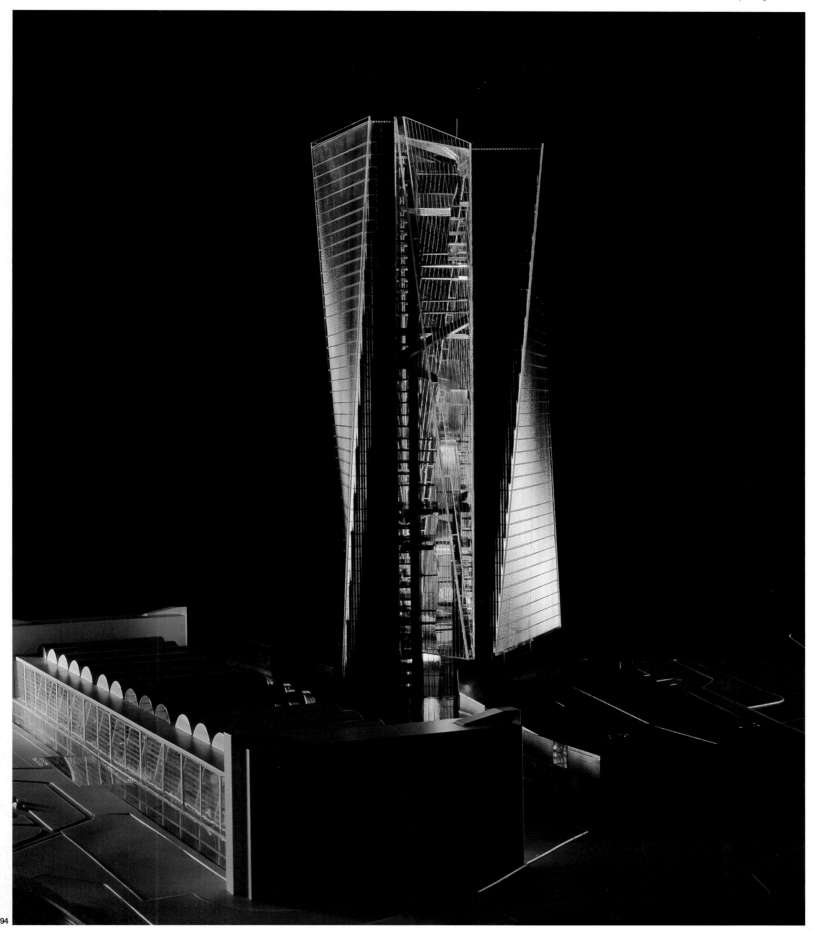

THE GREAT ARCH OF BEIJING

195. **Project (under construction) for the headquarters of CCTV in Beijing, by Rem Koolhaas (OMA).** Set in the very heart of the city's business district, this hybrid is based on the principle of the loop. A hypersophisticated frame from Cecil Balmond underpins the 260-meter-tall arch.
On the same site OMA is putting up a hotel and convention centre: a smaller, flexible tower.

195

196

A NEW, SMALL GENERATION

196. **The Neue Zollhof office complex in Düsseldorf, Germany, by Frank Gehry.** This sculptural set of three separate buildings is the big attraction in this river port. Based on a plan like pieces of a puzzle, it is intended to break down the sheer visual massiveness of a 28,000-square-meter project: thus the diversity of form is matched by diversity of materials. Each with its own cladding – metal, plaster, brick – the three towers all have markedly projecting windows that help structure them around a central nucleus.

197. **Topeak Tower in Beijing, by Herzog&de Meuron.** On the corner of Beijing's second ring road, this group of mixed-function programmes creates its own personal silhouette. Three elements, three different shapes. Three small towers instead of one big one, adding up to a sculptural alternation of panels transparent and opaque.

197

WHITE GRID

198. **Accommodation and shops in Beijing, by Rikken Yamamoto and Mikan.** Right in the heart of Beijing's business district this Soho ("small office, home office") programme generates its own contemporary landscape: a series of identical towers – maximum height 100 metres and all with the same aspect – breaking through a grille in which shops, leisure facilities and parking lots are bathed in natural light. Harmony for the mix of public and private comes from the interplay of terraces and agreeably diversified spaces.

Following double-page spread.
CADAVRE EXQUIS

199>202. **Mixed-function building at Lyon Confluence, France, by Winy Maas (MVRDV), Van Eckeraat, Manuelle Gautrand, Marrec & Combarel.** Dutch developer ING is bringing a new kind of town planning to its area of the peninsula between the Rhône and Saône rivers in Lyon. The "macroblock" of 30,000 square metres is half offices and half housing, with the emphasis on diversity. In this very compact project the private housing is complemented by four social housing briefs, one devoted to handicapped people. Four architects are contributing, each with his own section and style: brick for Winy Maas, wood for Van Eckeraat, textured concrete for Manuelle Gautrand, and Ductal for Marrec & Combarel (detail of the facade bottom page 223). The same materials are also being featured in the block's semi-public space.

ed 681 proposals in 1971). Ideas came in from 63 countries, the winner being Michael Arad's, on the theme of Reflecting Absence. Here the presence of absence takes the form of two pools exactly matching the base areas of the towers and dug down to 10 metres below street level. Water transforms the space into a shrine. Ten years before, Libeskind's proposal for the former concentration camp of Oranienburg had used the same material – water – to drown without trace a place of memory.

The debate over memory can be paralleled with that over identical reconstruction of historically significant sites, one example being the cathedral in Dresden, just rebuilt stone for stone by international subscription. The issue here was the repair of war damage – not at all the same thing as Berlin Castle (dynamited after the war in what was then East Germany) or the Château des Tuileries in Paris, both of which have been controversially suggested for rebuilding.

The idea here is to re-establish lost historical truth. In Russia, Boris Yeltsin had Christ the Saviour's cathedral rebuilt on its original site in Moscow: a more than justifiable step, but which had the unfortunate effect of doing away with the Moskva swimming pool, a circle 130 metres in diameter and one of the handsomest modern examples of the genre ever built.

A new generation of public space

In his *Non-Places: Introduction to an Anthropology of Supermodernity*, Marc Augé alerts us to the proliferation of sites he sees as typifying the triteness of contemporary public spaces. His point of view coincides with that of Rem Koolhaas, who predicts, in his 2001 bible *Project in the City*, the ineluctable development of what he calls "junk space". Logically, he says, this product of the "meeting between air conditioning and the escalator", will result in the "endless building".

At the same time, however, the city is recovering its empty spaces and working on its abandoned zones. We are witness to a rise of interest in the public space – and not just with greening in mind. From Beirut to Volgograd to Montreal, the big thing is brownfield reclamation: industrial sites, ports, army barracks, whatever. Urban property is becoming a safe investment as the city and nature cuddle up ever closer. The Benagantil park in Alicante, Spain, completed in 2003 by French team Obras is both an illustration of the reclamation strategy and a key to new uses: on this hillside looking out to sea, a site in which local residents had lost all faith, the architects have established fresh breathing spaces.

Another welcome reversal has taken place in Berlin, where the Potsdamer Platz ensemble is set between two public spaces: on one side a lake offering agreeable mirror effects, on the other the planted slope of the Tilla-Durieux Park, an extended sculpture half-park and half-square. The intervening space is a consciously created "in between": in Berlin as elsewhere, the issue is turning handicaps into assets. And everywhere the trend is to positive handling of urban space: look at the way the Catalans know how to juggle with a city, with the park reclaimed by Sergi Godia Fran and Xavier Casas Galofré on the Barcelona fringe site of Llobregat (1998).

In the reclamation field, there is one perfect and literal example of transformation: the garbage dump become park. This was the challenge taken up by architects Roig & Battle 20 kilometres southwest of Barcelona, where the unofficial Deposito de la Vall d'en Joan is now a zigzag-inspired place to relax and take a stroll. And even if the limitless public space of the Barcelona Forum goes totally counter to the local culture, it remains a symbol of this policy of reclamation, covering, in passing, the roof of a waste treatment plant.

In the dynamic of flows and links, a new generation of public spaces is coming to light, as the keywords of the modern city – interface, intermodality, in between – create places that generate intense urban activity, and mechanisms conducive to all kinds of urban practises amid the communication flows and nodes. The enormous traffic circle on the Plaça las Glòries is looking ripe for demolition

199

200

201

202

203

MINIMAL INTERVENTION

203+204. **Winning project for the Acropolis Museum in Athens, by Bernard Tschumi.** Standing 300 metres below the Acropolis, the museum will notably be home to the celebrated friezes of the Parthenon. The project offers a fulltime visual relationship with the ancient hilltop, giving the visitor as much as it can without actually touching the ruins. Standing on a forest of micropiles set amid ruins, the museum is determinedly minimalist, the idea being to maintain for the public an atmosphere based on four elements only: marble, concrete, glass and natural light. The layout generates a three-dimensional loop running from the remains to the friezes.

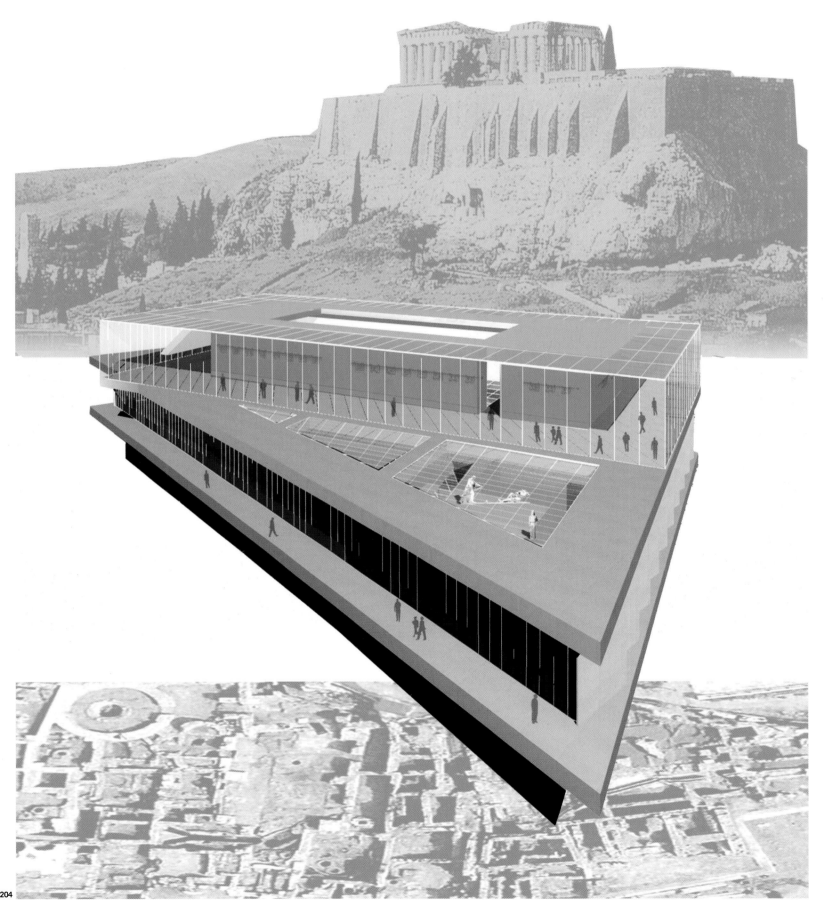

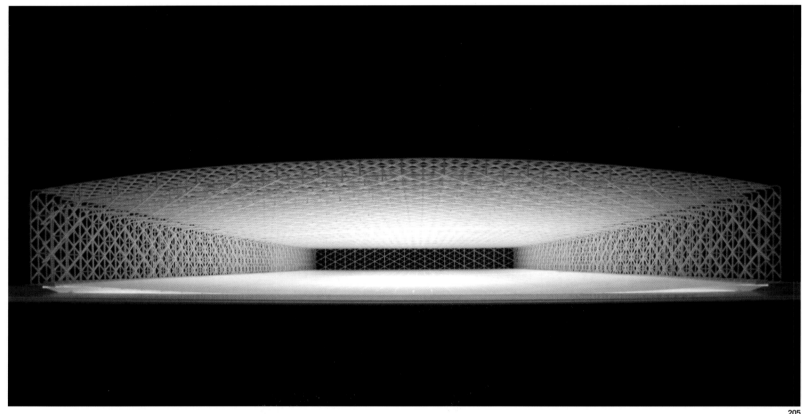

205

PERFORATED PLAQUE

205+206. **The winning project for the Design Centre in Saint-Etienne, France, by Finn Geipel (Lin).** Symbolic of the change the city has undergone, this contemporary element has been added to the site of the old arms manufactory. This pure, radical graft – a long, perforated plaque – is intended to be interactive. Its envelope is a variable skin designed to adapt to changing programmes and provide different interior ambiences. The project is complemented by a signal, a small metal-mesh tower offering a view of the site.

Following double page spread.

MINERAL-VEGETAL

207. **Winning project for the Quai Branly Museum in Paris, by Jean Nouvel.** A bridge flung out over an extensive garden, this Primitive Art museum reflects its designer's choice of a "presence/absence" theme. The garden is the work of landscape artist Gilles Clément. From the Quai Branly the building itself is all but invisible, silkscreened glass barriers barely allowing a view of the suspended boxes projecting from the facade. To ensure ultimate integration, the hypersophisticated building links up to the local Haussmann edifices via a green wall, designed by botanist Patrick Blanc and comprising 1,500 plants. The roof, visible from the Eiffel Tower, has ponds that make it an agreeable setting for a restaurant.

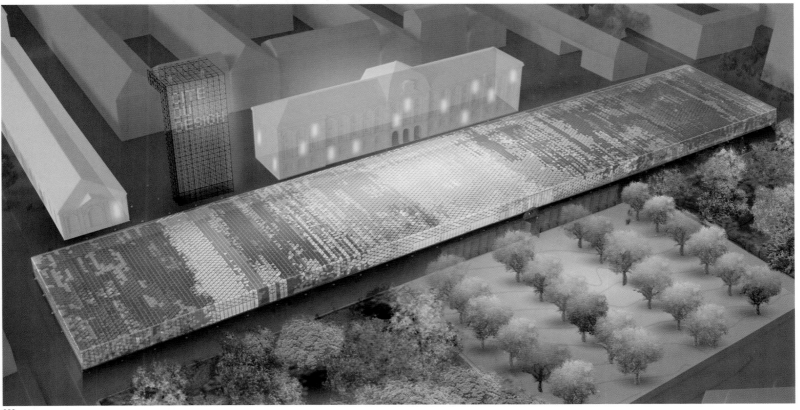

206

208

SWIMMING SPOT

208+209. Islands Brygge, public space in the port of Copenhagen, by Julien de Smedt & Bjarke Ingels (Plot).
Development of the Danish capital's waterside towards the north of the city has meant an opportunity to create new urban spaces: in this case, a public swimming spot that is not a pool in the sporting sense, but a convivial, playful outdoor space. With its landscape of wooden terraces, this group of four pools – 1,600 square metres in all – is designed as an extension of a park.

209

THE ROOF AS AN ACTIVE ELEMENT
210+211. **A youth and sailing club in Copenhagen, by Plot.**
The challenge posed by the brief was the combining of
two not really complementary – and even contradictory –
functions. The architects reacted with a project based on
the distortion of a surface: wood decking used as ground
and roof succeeds in reconciling the activities.

for lack of use of the park at its centre; but the huge Nudo de la Trinitat park/junction – 2 kilometres in diameter – developed north of Barcelona by Roig & Battle is a model of adaptation to infrastructures, with nature finding its niche in the heart of a network of expressways.

The park idea can also be understood in territorial terms. A convincing example comes from the Ruhr, where the Emscher Park Internationale Bau-Ausstellung (International Building Exhibition), launched in the 90s is an emblem of the determination to convert an entire region. Germany's black country has gone green, driven by a series of town planning, architecture and landscaping projects in upwards of 90 different municipalities. One result is that the Radweg, or cycle path, has become the mining country's unifying thread.

Nor should we forget Faliron, on the Athens shoreline. A two-kilometre stretch of the city's historic port was left deserted for decades after this natural access to the sea was cut by an urban motorway, and it was only the prospect of the 2004 Olympics that led the Greek authorities to put an end to this non-place. After an international workshop had been held, Bernard Reichen designed a new urban space, open to pedestrians and boat traffic alike. The Olympic beach volleyball competition is over, but

the reclaimed site lives on, and with a tramline into the bargain.

Together with these ripostes and the new opportunities they offer city dwellers, other public spaces are appearing, generating new modes of urban use. In the port at Copenhagen, for example, young architects Plot are offering a space that is clearly out to escape both the established order and privatisation. Overtly laying claim to public status, this bathing spot in the middle of the city is everything but a swimming pool or boating club: it's just a place where you can peel off and cool off, just as people do in the pools in Paris's Trocadéro gardens every summer.

Change has come to the walkway, too, and the latest feats – among them Calatrava in Bilbao, Foster & Caro in London, Rudi Ricciotti in Seoul – really deserve the dual title of work of art and public space. In Paris the Solférino footbridge linking the Musée d'Orsay and the Tuileries gardens (2000) is no banal crossing point: it's a meeting place for two riverbanks, two different levels and two different flows. The crossing takes place very elegantly at the junction of two arches forming a public square over the Seine. Marc Mimram, its creator, went on to design a footbridge in Strasbourg (2004), using the same suspended square concepts. Paris is currently awaiting Dietmar Feichtinger's footbridge, all visual suppleness, between the Bibliothèque Nationale and the

Parc de Bercy: a triple loop whose calculated touches of urbanity will include secondhand booksellers and flower vendors. Graz, in Austria, now has its unidentified floating object: artist Vito Acconci's bridge on the river Mur is a cultural hybrid that includes a café and a theatre.

Towers and more towers

Urban populations are endlessly on the rise. By 2007, according to a United Nations study, more than one person in every two on our planet will be a city-dweller: 5 billion in the cities, 3 billion in the country. The megalopolis is a big trend too: there will be thirty of them by 2015, several with over 20 million people: Bombay, Mexico City, New Delhi, New York, São Paulo and, biggest of all, Tokyo. In this kind of landscape the return of the tower seems inevitable.

Debate on the issue is still vigorous, notably given the relevance of whether or not to build upwards rather than outwards. The 9/11 terrorist attack that made a martyr of Manhattan has changed nothing at all and the race for the height record seems to be on again – as if there could be no question of lowering our guard, of giving the impression that the modern world might be afraid. True, certain tower projects have been cancelled or provisionally put on ice; but mainly for financial reasons.

210

211

212

213

214

215

HILL AS AGORA
212>219. Benagantil Park in Alicante, Spain, by Marc Bigornet and Fréderic Bonnet (Obras).
Triggered by a Europan competition, this development project for a hill between the city and the sea is a fine example of how to reverse a situation: the abandoned site was brought back to life by measures based on the notion of change that left everything in place. "Interweaving different scales of what can be perceived with the senses", the park's series of sequences make it a meeting point by the sea.

216

217

218

219

220

SEASHELLS IN THE DUNES
220+221. **Project for the Parque de la Relajacion at Torrevieja, Spain, by Toyo Ito.** This park is a leisure venue that fits with the growth of health tourism. The driving notion is integration into the environment, and to achieve this the architect has created waves in the landscape, gently treating a hill as if it were a dune covered with ripples of sand. This rationale leads naturally to the organic world of seashells, with the main frame of steel and wood taking on a spiral movement.

222

Acutely conscious that it was falling behind other European metropolises, Paris has set the debate going again. Two stances are worth noting here: Jean Nouvel's "acupuncture", with handsome objects set here and there in strategic spots; and Dominique Perrault's idea of building towers where there are already towers. A sculptural approach or a contextual one? It appears a very French debate for some commentators, who point out that in the long run economics will decide.

The fascination with superstructure remains. "A vertical blind alley," says Paul Virilio of the tower. The object itself isn't dead, but it needs redefining. There's already more technology, as in the Times Square media buildings in New York, but what people also want is more social variety and more ecology. Profitability is no longer the sole criterion.

This is a time of new tower concepts: Jean Nouvel's Agbar Tower in Barcelona, with a double skin that frees users from the air-conditioning trap; the Coop Himmelb(l)au tower in Frankfurt, for the European Central Bank; Norman Foster's Swiss Re in London, a model of hyper-sophistication; also in London, the Shard of Glass, Europe's tallest at 310 metres – a multifunctional design by Renzo Piano, with a raised piazza as a distinctive feature. And coming soon to Beijing is the "Chinese Loop", the CCTV tower designed by Koolhaas's OMA: with credits already including the 1996 Bangkok "Hyperbuilding", Koolhaas is getting ready to provide the Chinese capital with an XXL hybrid, a sort of giant arch of the third kind worked up by his associate, structural engineer Cecil Balmond.

A new concept has come along with Dominique Perrault's folded tower for Donau City in Vienna, a kaleidoscopic 200-metre object intended to dialogue with the Herzog & de Meuron organic tower in the heart of the Austrian capital. The French architect's sculptural structure will seem to change shape in line with changes in the light. Interestingly, in the same city Massimiliano Fuksas has already set about this type of transformation with the Wienerberger headquarters (2001), twin towers that look different from each other according to the play of light. Over and above this aesthetic agenda, it is notable that these crystalline towers – they have no spandrels at all – are set directly on their plinths: here the tertiary sector is directly connected to retail and leisure strata.

FLYING LEAF

222. **The Praça do Patriarca public space in Sao Paulo, Brazil, by Mendes da Rocha.** How to make an architectural statement with a square set on a viaduct in the heart of the city. Formerly the square had been ignored, serving as a bus station; now it is a pedestrian area and the exit – under a massive structure of white steel – for an underground passageway. The system uses a 40-meter-wide portico to hold up the protective canopy: a skilled use of equilibrium between the horizontal arch and this fine, handsomely curved leaf.

Facing page.
GREAT WAVES

223. **The Diagonal del Mar park in Barcelona, by Miralles & Tagliabue.** Part of the extension of the great thoroughfare towards the sea – punctuated along the way by the blue triangle of Herzog & de Meuron's Barcelona Forum – this botanically sustainable park is full of affectionate nudge-winks towards Gaudi (the ironwork, the hanging ceramic jars) and its own freedom of form. The pathways, for example, spread like the branches of a tree, ensuring the connection with the city. Set around an informal lake, the public space is marked by large metal structures, undulating metal pergolas that lash at the Catalan sky.

223

224

ARCHITECTURE AS EVENT
224+225. **Project for a retail and leisure area in Guadalajara, Mexico, by Coop Himmelb(l)au.** In 1998 the Mexican city launched a major urban project with a host of international stars including Philip Johnson, Toyo Ito, Zaha Hadid, Daniel Libeskind, Tom Mayne and Jean Nouvel. The Viennese team got the job of building a play-inflected shopping mall, under whose vast expressionist canopy new kinds of spaces are taking shape.

225

227

Facing page.
FLOATING MESH
226. **Footbridge over the river Mur at Graz, Austria, by artist Vito Acconci.** This hybrid work does not settle for linking the two banks of the river: it also offers an urban space with a café, a 200-seat theatre and facilities for children. Described by the New York artist as being "as fluid as water", the footbridge emerged from the deforming of a double geodesic dome. Floating on the water, the glass-faceted metal nest is attached to the banks by two more classical footbridges.

MOBILE AND SLENDER
227. **Mobile footbridge in Buenos Aires, Argentina, by Santiago Calatrava.** As part of the conversion of the brick-built docks at Puerto Madeiro, the Spanish architect-engineer created a discreet link: not so much a technical feat as the urge to set up a dialogue between the mobile footbridge and the disused cranes of the docks.

228

229

230

CRYSTALLINE AND CRAZY
228>230. **Bridge House at Middleburg, Holland, by Bar.**
Everything in this little building is devoted to mobility.
Entirely prefabricated and brought in by boat, it is installed
on a canal and functions mainly as the command centre
for a mobile footbridge. All the rest is pure aesthetics.
Fixed to its concrete base like a sculpture on its pedestal,
the glass house is a perfect equilateral triangle
whose steel frame is covered with a crystalline skin.

231

WHEN STRUCTURE MEANS ITINERARY
231. **Pair of road bridges at Teda, China, by Marc Mimram.**
One of the founding acts for a fast-growing new city, these
two parallel bridges vault the freeway coming from Beijing.
Their architect-engineer creator has long been exploring
ways of breaking elements down in concrete form: here
the organic vocabulary of the open leaves is evocative of
palms.

Facing page.
232. **Footbridge over the Rhine at Kehl, linking France and
Germany, by Marc Mimram.** More than just a bridge, this is
a pleasure spot for pedestrians and cyclists. The link is
achieved by superposition of two decks: a 270-metre arch
between the two banks and a flat arch of 400 metres
linking two public gardens.

A new housing development landscape

Did someone say urban sprawl? Looking beyond America's 20,000 gated communities – total population 8 million – we find a new kind of housing development appearing.

After Stuttgart's famed Weissenhof residential estate of the 1920s and the Berlin International Building Exhibition of the 50s, with Gropius, Aalto, Le Corbusier and others, the 90s saw the emergence of what could be considered "architecture parks". At Fukuoka in southern Japan, Arata Isozaki brought together a glittering array of architects that included Rem Koolhaas, Steven Holl and Christian de Portzamparc, to build apartment buildings around him, strictly in the spirit of the luxury development. China has picked up on the famous-name syndrome and a private developer has chosen a dozen Asian stars, among them Shigeru Ban, Kengo Kuma and Cui Kai, to build dream houses at the foot of the Great Wall. Another investor has launched a programme for 2005 bringing together ten Chinese and ten non-Chinese architects – including Cui Kai from China, Mathias Klotz from Chile, Alberto Kalach from Mexico, Sejima from Japan, and Odile Decq from France – to shape a new contemporary lakeside landscape.

In the domain of the housing development as such, two types of experiment stand out. Firstly MVRDV's Hagen Island operation in Holland: in this archipelago with the emphasis on diversity the aim is to create different environments via the interplay of sites, colours and materials.

France too sees itself as a laboratory. At Rézé, not far from Nantes, the members of the Périphériques group have suggested a new set of rules for a housing development, stressing architectural diversity as a way of stimulating social variety and banishing predictability. At Mulhouse, Jean Nouvel has taken over planning of the exemplary "Manifesto City" operation, to which several teams – Shigeru Ban, Duncan Lewis, Lacaton & Vassal, with the extrapolation from their inhabitable greenhouse concept, and others – have already brought their ideas on alternative housing. The concern here is to achieve stylistic diversity while ensuring that each domestic space cultivates a half-indoor/half-outdoor ambiguity, with vegetation sometimes called in to help.

Providing more than French public housing standards call for: this was the outcome of a demonstration kicked off by Lacaton & Vassal with their Latapie house at Floirac, in the

232

suburbs of Bordeaux. The challenge was simple: maximum results with a minimum budget, and they came out with more space at low cost. This was proof that public housing, once an architecture laboratory in its own right, can still be exploratory. Even if, for the moment, fixed standards have nipped experimentation in the bud.

Nomadism and urbanism

Our time is also marked by the emergence of alternative architectures, rendered atypical by force of circumstance or the need to adapt to a difficult economic and social context. Today urbanism and nomadism go hand in hand. The creative world has proved capable of adapting to this changed urban usage: artists like the New Yorker Wodiczko, designers like leading "mobile unit" specialist Joep Van Lieshout – and architects.

François Roche and his mobile, furtive housing tested on the streets of Paris in 1998;

Manuel Tardits and his itinerant web café in Tokyo (Mikan, 1998); Grégoire & Petetin and their suitcase-house for Berlin (1997); Richard Horden's Alpine Ski Haus, a skiers' refuge derived from the helicopter; Didier Faustino of the Bureau des Mésarchitectures and the strange floating theatre he designed for Expo 02 in Switzerland; and the Toro Lab group from Mexico, with its printed nomadic shelter that also works as a visiting card. Architecture comes in all sorts of portable – and light – versions, such as the lookout-house keeping an eye on the port in Rotterdam: like a limpet clinging to its rock, the "Parasite" hung on the famous Las Palmas warehouse is one with its 1920s host. Cutting free of the rules and cultivating ephemera that like to last, architects Korteknie & Stuhlmacher have devised a soft green structure, entirely in wood, now moored to Bakema's disused building.

By way of proof temporary architecture-gives rise to smart projects; The bicycle facility built in 2002 by VMX in the harbour of

Amsterdam is a good combination af infrastructure and architecture; The 100 metre long steel overhang structure is composed of a series of ramps conceived for the storage of 2,500 bikes. And let's spare a wistful thought for the late Otto Steidle, who set out across the Alps from Munich for the Venice Biennale aboard his "nomadic tower". A low-tech manifesto if ever there was one.

Since then, the idea of mobile architecture has spread more and more. In Paris in 2001 Karine Hermann and Jérôme Sigwalt created the "mezzanine on wheels" as monumental piece of furniture, actually a 15 square meter office moving in a photographer's studio. In Utrecht, Korteknie & Stuhlmacher imagined in 2004 the mobile artist's studio; This wooden architecture combines a place to stay and a place to work, with shifting facades.

But the peak of nomadism is reached by Shigeru Ban with the Nomadic Musem. Instead of moving the museum throughout the world, the Japanese architect offers to move the concept. It only remains to hire a whole battery of containers in order to build 200 metre long walls (by 15 metre high). Maybe it is the cheapest of the large buildings with its paper tubes colonnade supporting the textile roof. With his "containerised" museum Shigeru Ban puts much emphasis on a fundamental point: there is no difference between permanent and temporary architecture. It is always a matter of work and a consideration for a society eager for new experiments.

233

234

235

236

THE LOW-COST AESTHETIC
233>236. **Nomadic Museum by Shigeru Ban.** With containers as its starting point, this cultural facility is based on the most standardised element in the world. 200 metres long and 25 metres wide, this unit was set up for the first time in New York in 2004, and can be put together anywhere in the world: all a city has to do is put in a request. A textile roof held up by a colonnade of cardboard tubes covers the totally dismountable, totally cost-effective structure.

Facing page.
WALKING MANIFESTO
237. **The "Nomad Tower" installation for the 2000 Venice Biennale, by Otto Steidle.** In response to a call by Massimiliano Fuksas, the Venice Biennale curator in 2000, the Munich architect designed this mobile unit: a building made to go on the road. The Tower has messages to transmit, showing films on such contradictory binomes as high tech/low tech, heavy/light, transparent/opaque, lasting/ephemeral and formal/informal – all of them core issues in architectural debate today.

238

MOBILE PLATFORM

238+239. **A mobile artist's studio in Utrecht, Holland, by Korteknie & Stuhlmacher.** Situated out where the city and the country meet, itinerant abode Number 19 is the address of an artist – in – residence. As an example of nomadic architecture, it is designed to be moved as one piece. Mostly wood – with a few metal reinforcements – the studio is a long black box that captures the light. The front facade of this artistic container opens up completely, allowing the inside to be used for exhibition purposes.

239

Photographic credits

© **Acconci Studio** : p. 242
© **Agence Lin - images BSY/SCD** : p. 48, 226, 227
© **Agence Mimram** : p. 247
© **Atelier BOW-WOW** : p. 138
© **Atelier Christian De Portzamparc** : p. 78-79, 80, 81, 164, 165
© **Binet Hélène** : p. 96
© **Bitter Jan** : p. 30-31, 162, 163
© **Bitter Jan & Kisling Anette** : p. 193, 194, 195
© **Blengini Giuseppe** : p. 64, 65
© **Boeri Stefano** : p. 97
© **Borel Nicolas** : p. 87
© **Bousema Anne / Stuhlmacher Korteknie** : p. 9
© **Cardelus David** : p. 85
© **Chaix & Morel** : p. 23
© **Colboc et Franzen** : p. 100
© **Combarel & Marrec** : p. 141, 182-183
© **Coop Himme(l)blau** : p. 56, 72, 73, 240, 241
© **Cuisset Thibaut** : p. 18
© **Decq Odile & Cornette Benoit** : p. 172, 173, 184, 185
© **Diller et Scofidio + Rento** : p. 44, 45
© **Diller et Scofidio** : p. 117
© **Duccio Malamba** : p. 34-35, 36, 37
© **Faustino Didier / Bureau des Mésarchitectures** : p. 46, 152
© **Ferreira Alves Luis** : p. 136, 137
© **Fessy Georges** : p. 74, 75, 102, 103, 200, 201
© **Fessy Georges, MDA IBOS-VITART** : p. 24, 25
© **Ferrier Jacques** : p. 158
© **F.O.A.** : p. 145, 178
© **Fuksas Massimiliano** : p. 104-105
© **Herault Arnaud architectes** : p. 196
© **Hertzog et de Meuron** : p. 202, 203, 219
© **Hiro Sakugushi** : p. 71
© **Galvez Pérez Maria** : p. 94
© **Gautrand Manuele** : p. 179
© **Geninasca Delefortrie SA, Architectes FASSIA** : p. 14-15
© **Jaque Andrés** : p. 120, 121
© **Jakob & MacFarlane** : p. 154
© **KKAA** : p. 68, 69
© **Kahl Christian** : p. 250, 251
© **Kapoor Anish / Tate Modern** : p. 106
© **Kitajima Toshiharu** : p. 180, 181
© **Knauf Holger, Düssendorf** : p. 170, 171
© **Kramer Luuk** : p. 156
© **Liebeskind Daniel** : p. 57
© **MADA s.p.a.m** : p. 19
© **Loub Stefan** : p. 214
© **Leppert Quirin / Wirtgen Steffen** : p. 132, 133
© **Lewis Duncan** : p. 50, 51
© **Mansilla & Tuñón arquitectos** : p. 26-27, 82-83, 84

© **Martinez Eduardo** : p. 89
© **Maas Winny (MRDV, Van Echeraat, Gautrand Manuele, Marrek & Combarel)** : p. 222-223
© **Monolab Architects** : p. 139
© **Monthiers Jean-Marie** : p. 124, 125
© **Moran Michael** : p. 248
© **Morin André** : p. 159
© **Musch Jeroen** : p. 95
© **Nacàsa & Partners inc** : p. 10, 11
© **Nikolis Monika** : p. 110, 111, 112-113
© **Nio-Architèkten** : p. 91
© **Nouvel Jean** : p. 60, 212, 213, 228-229
© **OAL / Édouard François** : p. 126
© **OBRAS** : p. 234, 235
© **OMA** : p. 216-217
© **ONL [Oosterhuis_Léonárd]** : p. 42, 43 (top and bottom)
© **Osorio Carlos** : p. 88
© **Pattist Hans** : p. 186, 187
© **Perrault Dominique / ADAGP-Paris 2005** : p. 12, 58, 59
© **Piano Renzo** : p. 210, 211
© **PLOT** : p. 169, 230, 231, 233
© **Poitevin M. / Maupin S. / Sans J.** : p. 192
© **R & Sie** : p. 115, 116, 146, 147
© **Rambert Francis** : p. 16, 17, 40, 41, 47, 54, 55, 61, 62, 63 (top, bottom left, bottom right), 76-77, 92, 93, 107, 130, 131, 140, 142-143, 175, 176, 177, 218, 221, 238, 239, 243, 246, 249
© **Ricciotti Rudy** : p. 197, 204, 205
© **Richard Johnson / Interior Images** : p. 71
© **Richters Christian** : p. 28, 29, 122, 123
© **Richters Christian / NL Embassy** : p. 174
© **Rob't Hart** : p. 101, 148-149, 155, 244, 245
© **Ruault Philippe** : p. 38-39, 127 (top and bottom), 134, 135, 160, 161, 198, 199
© **SANAA** : p. 13, 66-67
© **Scanarello Adelfo** : p. 32, 33
© **Smoothy Paul** : p. 128, 129
© **Souto Moura - Architectos, LDA** : p. 20, 21
© **Suzuki Hisao** : p. 188, 189
© **Tchumi Bernard** : p. 224, 225
© **Toyo ITO & Associates** : p. 118-119, 236, 237
© **Un Studio** : p. 73, 166-167, 168
© **van Leeuwen Hans** : p. 157
© **Walti Ruedi** : p. 150, 151
© **Young Nigel / Foster and Partners** : p. 8
© **Zaha Hadid Architects** : p. 190-191, 191
© **Zaha Hadid, Araka Isozaki, Daniel Libeskind, Pier Paolo Maggiora** : p. 208-209
© **Zugmann Gerald** : p. 215
© **DR** : p. 55

Printed by Eurografica, Vicenza, Italy. October 2005